COMFORT BAKES

COMFORT BAKES

George Hepher

80 Seriously Good Cakes, Bakes and Treats for Every Craving

CONTENTS

INTRODUCTION — 6
KITCHEN MUST-HAVES — 9
FAQS — 12

SAUCES + DRIZZLES — 16

Caramels — 21
Lemon Curd — 25
Sticky Toffee Sauce — 26
Custard, Three Ways — 29
Chocolate Fudge Sauce — 31

EASY LIKE SUNDAY MORNING — 32

Chocolate Rocky Road Tower — 37
Millionaire's Shortbread — 38
Ultimate Blondies — 39
Strawberry Milkshake Cookies — 40
Oat + Choc Chip Cookies — 41
Pumpkin Spice + Caramelized White Chocolate Cookies — 44
Seashell Brownies — 47
Peanut Butter Crispy Clusters — 48
Galaxy Caramel Lump — 51
Biscoff Blondies — 52
Pumpkin Spice Cake — 55
Chocolate Cookie Dough — 56
Almond Croissant Loaf Cake — 59
Cookie Cereal — 60

BAKING TO SHARE 62

Salted Caramel Cornflake Rocky Road 66
Milkybar + Mini Egg Cookie Millionaires 69
Nutella Brownies 70
Churros Blondies 73
Earl Grey + Lavender Cake 74
Blondie Roll 77
Raspberry Ripple Cheesecake Sandwiches 78
Raspberry + Lemon Cheesecake Blondies 80
Triple Chocolate Cornflake Roll 83
Peaches + Cream Stuffed Thiccc Cookies 84
Pistachio Cookie Millionaires 87

ULTIMATE CROWD PLEASERS 88

Milkybar Funfetti Cookie Sandwiches 93
Pistachio Rolls 94
Millionaire's Shortbread Cheesecake 96
Sticky Toffee Tart 99
Pistachio Tart 100
Pecan Pie + Salted Caramel Cake 103
Piña Colada Pie 105
Biscoff Rocky Road Cheesecake 109
Apple Pie + Custard Cake 110
Dairy Milk Millionaire Brownie 113
Blueberry + Lemon Cheesecake Cake 115

SNUG SAVOURIES 116

Shortcrust Pastry Case 120
Puff Pastry 121
Quiche Lorraine 123
Pear, Prosciutto, Gorgonzola + Walnut Quiche 124
Caprese Quiche 126
Roasted Grape and Goat's Cheese Scones 127
Pizza Focaccia 129
Harissa Sausage Rolls 131
Cranberry, Brie + Bacon Rolls 132
Air Fryer Spring Rolls 135
Wild Garlic, Spinach, Ricotta + Lancashire Cheese Puffs 137
Cheese Biscuits 141
Pumpkin, Walnut, Sausage + Blue Cheese Pies 143
Roasted Fig, Prosciutto + Truffle Boursin Tart 144
Hot Honey, Jalapeño + Cheesy Garlic Knots 147

INDULGENT PUDDINGS 148

Pistachio Tiramisu 152
Baked Cookie Dough 157
Raspberry Ombré Cheesecake Cake 158
Baileys Custard Tart 162
Apple Crumble + Custard Cheesecake 165
Biscoff Poke Cake 166
Triple Chocolate Brownie Cake 167
Sour Cherry + Chocolate Gelato Cake 171
Snickers Cake 173

COSY FAVOURITES 174

Spotted Dick Traybake 178
Espresso Martini Hot Fudge Brownie Sundae 179
Sticky Toffee Pudding 183
Carrot Cake 184
Chocolate Gelato 187
Treacle Tart 188
Chocolate Fudge Cookies 191
Salted Caramel Cornflake Sandwiches 192
Tahini, Dark Chocolate + Sesame Cookies 195
Chocolate Orange Loaf Cake 196
Plum Crumble Cake 198
Toasted Honey, Pear + Cinnamon Cake 201

ACKNOWLEDGEMENTS 202
INDEX 204

Introduction

Well, you all lapped up *Rebel Bakes* and I've got to fund the lifestyle somehow, so here I am again, tip-tap-typing away at another book, and this time, it's all about comfort! Picture this. You're reclining on a chaise longue with a ladle in one hand and a rich, creamy tiramisu in the other whilst a Karen Huger three-wick engulfs the room. That refreshing bite into a fruity, chewy cookie on a beautiful summer's evening. Pacing around a sweet-scented oven in your slippers waiting – impatiently – for your favourite pudding to cook, whilst sipping on a glass of wine like Olivia Pope… This is very much the vibes of the recipes in this book, albeit with my own signature twist.

To me, when it comes to comfort baking, you're out of the pant suit and into your favourite cosy pyjamas, sipping on a cup of tea (I like overpriced herbal ones) and taking your time – something I hope this book embraces. All of the recipes have been selected with simplicity in mind, though a few of them have several steps that are best broken down over a slow weekend or a few days for maximum ease.

What with me still being so youthful (and one of the top 250 baking bachelors in central Cambridgeshire), my only real-life experiences are having my own business and being in full-time education. While I liked being creative at school (I once won our talent competition with a comedic acrobatic dance routine to Miley Cyrus's 'Wrecking Ball', shooting B-roll footage smashing polystyrene walls in my parents' conservatory), I was much more academic day-to-day. The weekends were my creative time: I spent many of them at home, baking and binge-watching movies and tv shows. For most of the year, the baking was pretty standard and an easy way to keep me occupied, until Christmas came around and I would turn into an entirely different person. My Christmas list gets written after I've planned what I'm cooking and baking for pretty much the whole month of December. *Nigella Christmas* would become sacred text to me. I must've made everything from the book at least three times – I hope my recipes become staples like this – and after every festive feast, I upped the ante with my bakes year-on-year. Once I started George's Bakery, I only had more time (and reason) to create new recipes and make playful interpretations of nostalgic classics as well as brand new creations, which I've compiled just for this book – lucky you…

Inside you'll find a delicious mix of comforting bakes, from super simple one-bowl treats perfect for a slow Sunday morning to fudgy, indulgent cakes and snug savouries to share with family and friends. Whether you're looking for a timeless favourite or something new to warm your kitchen, these recipes are designed to bring joy and warmth with every bite.

Happy baking! x

KITCHEN MUST-HAVES

First things first, I'm a self-confessed kitchenware and food snob, so from ingredients to utensils, I always want to use the branded and the best. However, this isn't at all essential, I've just been enabled with easy access to snazzy kitchen gadgets because my father owns an electrical appliance store. I was being gifted state-of-the-art food processors by my 10th birthday because I refused to bash biscuits wrapped in a tea towel for a cheesecake base, so I have an inflated sense of requirement. That said, if I can't get it for cost price, I'm not above 'accidentally' denting a device or two to get some money off...

These tips are ones I do genuinely stand by though, and where I really rave about a product it's because it's never failed me!

BUTTER

It's always unsalted and softened unless I specifically state otherwise. Room temperature is what you're aiming for and call me Sabrina Carpenter because please, please, PLEASE don't use baking block or margarine! If using salted butter in sweet bakes, just make sure to halve any salt listed in the recipe.

VANILLA

We played down my vanilla bean paste elitism as best we could in *Rebel Bakes* but I've gone one step further (and I suppose farther, too) and I now get it imported from Tahiti for my own personal use. However, just standard supermarket vanilla bean paste will do the trick – it's what I use in the bakery, and you can get it for a reasonable price. I recommend using this over essence or extract for maximum taste. I even know someone who bulk-bought some to bake the recipes from book one.

SALT

Maldon salt flakes are a lifestyle to me at this point and I use them wherever I talk of salt. I always rate flakes higher than table salt. Also, let it be known that while salt is included in pretty much all of the savoury recipes in this book, it's always best to season as you go for personal preference – I adore a salty mouthful, so even blue cheese is gonna need a sprinkling to me but we all have different palates!

EGGS

Large, room-temperature eggs are my go-to. Any talk of egg whites is roughly 40g (1½oz) per large egg and yolks are 20g (¾oz) per large egg.

FOOD COLOURINGS

Colour Mill is the best you can get, and it comes in every shade you can think of. It's oil based and a little goes a very long way – so even though it's pricier, I promise it can last years!

TINS

For any square traybakes, I'm a fan of Masterclass loose-bottomed tins as they're also an amazing depth and a lot of my recipes have layers upon layers! I've an aversion to spring-form tins (nobody wants an ugly rim...), as well as silicone bakeware, which tends to leave a thin, crumbly crust that really affects the structure of bakes. For cakes, I like a cheap supermarket 20cm (8") round tin but make sure to hand wash them otherwise their coating comes off very easily!

MEASURING SPOONS

A teaspoon is 5g and a tablespoon is 15g – avoid soup, bouillon or dessert spoons which can vary in capacity!

SPATULAS

Silicone spoon spatulas will change your life. I recommend opting for one with a stainless-steel core – although a little more expensive, you can scrape a bowl clean in seconds! Similarly, smaller 18cm (7") spatulas have even more spoonage and strength for the toughest of scrapings.

THERMOMETERS

A few of my recipes require a thermometer and I truly believe you won't have made your perfect brownie unless you've probed it, so a meat thermometer is a must have – old-school sugar thermometers are bulky, a kitchen eyesore and slower than a tortoise on tranquilizers.

ELECTRIC STAND MIXER

I collect KitchenAids like Jeremy Clarkson does cars and would highly recommend investing in an electric stand mixer for ease. Use a paddle attachment for beating or mixing, and a whisk for anything involving aeration and sugar syrups i.e. meringues or nougat, for example. However, if you want to keep things simple, old-fashioned electric whisks and mixing bowls with wooden spoons will also get the job done.

BEFORE YOU START BAKING...

Read through the recipe (and tips!) before getting started so you know exactly what you'll need when it all gets a bit everything everywhere all at once up in the kitchen! If you really want to be teacher's pet, have all of your ingredients weighed out before you start and always have your tin lined before you start any mixing.

FAQS

How's best to slice my bakes?

It can be really tricky to get the perfect cut on your bakes, especially as so many of my recipes require refrigerating and have chocolate toppings, but here's a few things you can do...

1. Remove the bake from the fridge and allow it to warm 30-45 minutes before slicing

2. Use a long, sharp knife that's larger than the traybake you're slicing

3. Heat the knife! Run the blade under hot running water before quickly drying off and slicing

4. Score the top of the traybake first so you know exactly where you need to cut

5. Clean the knife and run under hot water between every incision. Tedious, I know, but worth it for the perfect slice!

How's best to line my tins?

For round tins, place the base of the tin on greaseproof paper to draw around it and cut out. Grease the bottom of the tin and place the greaseproof on top. Grease the edges of the tin and cut greaseproof larger than the top of the tins and use this to line the edges.

For square tins, cut a piece of greaseproof paper larger than your tin. Grease the tin before pushing the greaseproof into the base. Create creases in the corners of the greaseproof and stick the edges to the sides. Use scissors to cut down the crease and unfurl the greaseproof corners, trimming off any excess.

How long should I leave my cakes to cool before icing?

Once your cakes have come out of the oven, I like to leave them to cool in the tins for about 30 minutes. If I'm ready to ice them straight away, I take them out of the tins and ice ahead, though if I want to wait, I'll wrap them in cling film and set aside for a couple of hours. You can also freeze the cakes once cooled and wrapped to thaw out and ice later.

What should I ice my cakes onto?

Now, I put very little effort into the icing of my cakes so just ice them onto a sheet of baking parchment, however, I'm blessed with large hands and a plethora of cake lifters to easily move my cakes about. If you're wanting to transport your cakes, it's best to use a cake board or drum (a drum is thicker and is really meant for tiered cakes) that's slightly larger than the circumference of your cake. For example, for a standard 20cm (8in) cake, look for a board that's 25cm (10in). If you're keeping it really simple, ice the cake straight onto a cake stand, just make sure you'll be able to easily decorate the sides.

How's best to store my bakes?

To make bakes last longer, I usually store them in an airtight container in the fridge and bring them back to room temperature before eating, where applicable. I say the general shelf life on bakes is 3 days for any containing fresh fruit or cream (including cheesecakes) and 5-7 days for most others, though let it be known brownies only improve after a week in the fridge in my mind.

Can I use vegetarian, vegan or halal marshmallows in your recipes?

Yes, you can substitute regular marshmallows for vegetarian, vegan or halal ones in my recipes but there's one main difference… they take a lot longer to melt! So, if they're being melted down in a recipe, my tips for this are to make sure you stir the mixture more frequently (to avoid any chocolate or other ingredients burning) or to chop them up finely. When chopping them, make sure you sprinkle the knife or scissors with icing sugar or cornflour to stop everything sticking together!

How can I sterilise jars to fill with sauces and give as gifts?

You need to sterilise jars before adding food to remove all of the bacteria, but it's really simple! Either wash jars in hot, soapy water before placing in an oven heated to 120°C/100°C fan/50°F/Gas ½ for 20 minutes, or place on a hot/intense cycle in the dishwasher before filling.

George, why are you obsessed with a bain-marie?

Here's what it is, you could and likely will use a microwave to melt your chocolate for rocky roads and ganaches, however, it makes it really likely to burn! So, to err on the side of caution, I prefer using a bain-marie (a bowl over a pan of barely simmering water) to reduce the risk, even if it takes a little longer! (Microwave the chocolate for the ganache in the triple choc cornflake roll recipe (page 83) though, otherwise you'll be waiting an hour to roll up your mixture!)

Why hasn't my cake risen?

First of all, it sure as hell ain't my recipe, so it must be you! Make sure not to overmix your cake batter, as this overdevelops the gluten, stopping the raising agents from working to their best potential. And check that you've used the correct quantities of bicarbonate of soda/baking powder. You may also be cooking the cake on too high a heat, or your tin is larger than required, so the batter is going sideways instead of upwards!

How can I make my cake gluten free?

It's a lot easier than you think! Swap the flour in the recipe to a gluten-free self-raising flour (my favourite brand is Doves Farm) and then add a couple of tablespoons of moisture to your batter (milk, lemon juice, flavourings, alcohol etc) to stop the cake drying out. It may be slightly crumblier when icing, so if you're concerned, wrap the cakes in cling film and refrigerate for 5 minutes before icing to avoid a crumbly mess.

Help! My cookies have spread too much!

Not to worry, you can use a large cookie cutter or any large round item to place over the cookie and swirl, pushing the cookie in on itself to create the perfect shaped cookie! It's likely happened because the cookie dough was too warm, causing the fat to spread too fast. To avoid this, make sure your batter is cool to the touch when rolling your dough balls before baking,

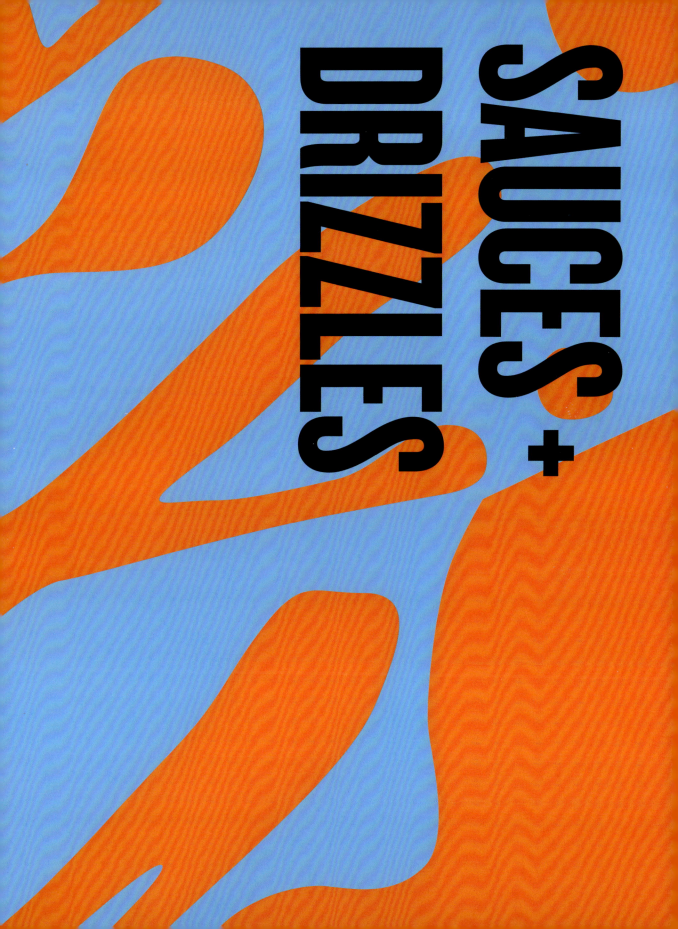

While most of the caramels, curds and custards in this chapter are just begging to be poured over a pudding or dessert, some are used as ingredients in their own right. All the sauces can be made ahead of time and heated through just before serving, while the curds and caramels make great gifts. Keep a stash of jars handy, ready to sterilize, to store any leftovers if you know won't be using the whole quantity in one go.

It was very hard not to repeat a few of the sauces from my first book, *Rebel Bakes*, because they're so incredible and widely used in my recipes. However, I've tarted them up a little for a bit of variation!

I should point out that there's really no reason why you can't drink a pint of custard on its own or pour several different sauces over one bake (custard with sausage rolls might taste weird, though) – the Sticky Toffee Pudding (see page 183) hits a little differently when served with both the Sticky Toffee Sauce (see page 26) and your pick from Custard, Three Ways (see page 29)!

Caramels	21
Lemon Curd	25
Sticky Toffee Sauce	26
Custard, Three Ways	29
Chocolate Fudge Sauce	31

CREAMY CARAMEL

This caramel is different in texture and flavour from my signature Thicc and Salted Caramel recipes (see pages 22 and 23). Think the inside of a caramel chocolate bar, but a little runnier – perfect for spreading between cake layers, drizzling onto bakes or just eating by the spoonful!

Prep + hob time:
20 minutes
Makes: 1kg (2lb 3oz)

450ml (15fl oz) double cream
1 tsp vanilla bean paste
½ tsp salt flakes
250g (9oz) liquid glucose
150g (5¼oz) caster sugar
150g (5¼oz) butter, softened

1. Heat the cream, vanilla and salt flakes in a saucepan over a medium heat until steaming, stirring occasionally.

2. Meanwhile, heat the liquid glucose and sugar in a separate saucepan over a medium-high heat, stirring occasionally, until the mixture reaches 180°C (350°F) and starts to turn golden.

3. Pour the cream mixture over the sugar and whisk to combine. Remove from the heat and allow the caramel to cool to 75°C (165°F), stirring occasionally, then whisk the butter through.

4. Allow to cool completely before decanting into jars and storing at room temperature for up to a week.

GEORGE LOVES A TIP!

— If your mixture looks lumpy after the cream mixture has been added to the sugar, either pass it through a sieve or continue to heat until the sugar lumps are completely dissolved.

Sauces + Drizzles

THICCC CARAMEL

Prep + hob time:
40 minutes
Makes: 1kg (2lb 3oz)

It's here again because it's just that good and is a component in so many of my bakes.

Ways we could improve on it from book one:
- Literally none, it really is perfect.

175g (6oz) butter
115g (4oz) light brown sugar
115g (4oz) golden syrup
750g (1lb 10oz) condensed milk

1. Put all your ingredients in a saucepan and start by stirring infrequently over a low heat with a spatula. Make sure to catch and break down any harder lumps of sugar while it dissolves and the butter is melting.

2. Once the butter and sugar have dissolved and are well combined, turn the heat up to medium-high.

3. Begin stirring continuously for 25–35 minutes (make sure the caramel doesn't catch on the bottom of the pan) until it begins to darken in colour. If you have a thermometer to hand, look for a temperature between 93–103°C (199–217°F). Another way to test if you're on the right track is by scooping up a teaspoon of the caramel and dropping a small amount into a glass of cold water. If a ball forms, your caramel is ready.

4. Take it off the heat but continue whisking for a couple of minutes to ensure that the residual heat in the pan doesn't burn or catch the caramel on the bottom.

Sauces + Drizzles

SALTED CARAMEL

Prep + hob time:
20 minutes
Makes: 1kg (2lb 3oz)

My Salted Caramel is the basis of many of my desserts and is also a great sauce in its own right. It will keep for at least a month in the fridge and makes a great gift.

450g (1lb) granulated sugar
200ml (6¾fl oz) double cream
250g (9oz) butter, diced
1 tsp salt flakes

1. Heat the sugar in a deep, heavy-bottomed saucepan over a medium-high heat, without stirring, until the sugar begins to melt.

2. Meanwhile pour the cream into a separate saucepan and warm over a low heat until steaming. Don't let it simmer!

3. When the sugar begins to melt, gradually stir with a spatula, bringing any lumps from around the edges to the centre of the pan so that the sugar melts evenly and begins to caramelize. Stir frequently until the sugar has completely melted and started to turn an amber colour.

4. Reduce the heat to low and add the butter to the sugar, a few cubes at a time, whisking between additions (take care as the mixture will froth and bubble) until all the butter is incorporated.

5. Slowly whisk the warmed cream into the sugar and butter mixture, then add the salt and whisk again to combine. Remove from the heat and leave to cool.

GEORGE LOVES A TIP!

— Create a Rum Salted Caramel by adding 100ml (3fl oz) of dark rum with the salt in step 5. A spiced dark rum will give the best flavour.

— If you have any caramelized chunks stuck to your pan after pouring out your caramel, fill the pan with water and bring to the boil to make cleaning it easier.

— To store this caramel or even give it as a gift, sterilize a jar before pouring the cooled caramel inside and sealing. Store in a cool, dry place.

LEMON CURD

A great way to get a strong, fruity flavour into the layers of your bake is to make a quick curd, which is a lot easier than you might realize. My version is thicker and less sweet than most shop-bought versions and is perfect in my Raspberry + Lemon Cheesecake Blondies (see page 80). You can experiment with using other fruits in this recipe (orange, lemon, apple and blackberry are all my go-tos) and don't be afraid to drizzle your curd over desserts, mix it into overnight oats or porridge, or enjoy with a cheeseboard or grazing table.

Prep + hob time:
20 minutes
Makes: 250g (9oz)

100ml (3½fl oz) lemon juice
3 egg yolks
75g (2¾oz) caster sugar
50g (2oz) butter

1. Put the lemon juice, egg yolks and sugar into a heavy-bottomed saucepan over a medium heat. Heat for 10–15 minutes, stirring continuously with a spatula, until thickened enough to coat the back of the spatula.

2. Remove from the heat, add the butter and stir until the butter has fully melted and incorporated.

3. Leave to cool before transferring to an airtight container and storing in the fridge for up to one week, or preserve by pouring the curd into sterilized jars and storing in a cool, dry place for up to six months.

GEORGE LOVES A TIP!

— To make pineapple curd, simply swap the lemon juice for the same quantity of freshly squeezed pineapple juice. This will come in handy for the Piña Colada Pie on page 105.

STICKY TOFFEE SAUCE

Lemme tell you that the main hardship of writing a cookbook is testing all the recipes. To find the perfect sticky toffee sauce recipe, I had to create and taste 20… and that's a lot harder than you'd think! Date molasses, also known as date syrup, is the secret ingredient to making this sauce rich, without the treacle becoming overpowering and leaving an unpleasant aniseed taste in the mouth. It also makes for a sauce that isn't as sickly sweet as most others you'll find… meaning you can stomach more!

Prep + hob time: 20 minutes
Makes: 200g (7oz)

75g (2¾oz) light brown sugar
25g (1oz) date molasses
75g (2¾oz) double cream
125g (4½oz) butter
½ tsp salt flakes

1. Heat all the ingredients together into a heavy-bottomed saucepan over a medium heat, stirring occasionally, until everything melts together.
2. Turn the heat up to high and bring to the boil. Reduce to a simmer and let the sauce cook for 5 minutes before removing from the heat.

GEORGE LOVES A TIP!
— This sauce is best used within a couple of days (simply reheat in a saucepan before serving). Store in an airtight container in the fridge in the meantime.

Sauces + Drizzles

CUSTARD, THREE WAYS

Ah, custard. The ultimate comfort blanket for puddings everywhere. It's so good, I couldn't help but include three takes on this classic. My Rich Custard is a showstopper, even if I do say so myself. It's rich, smooth, creamy... I could go on. And my Baileys Custard is great at Christmas when you want to doze off after dinner, although tolerances may vary (one of the bakery babes nearly fell off her bike and into a bush on the way home after trying a tablespoon of this) – you have been warned. For a beautifully spiced custard that pairs perfectly with an oaty apple crumble (or just about any dessert you want to elevate), this Chai Latte Custard is as simple as teabagging the cream and milk for five minutes and letting the flavours of cinnamon, cardamom and ginger infuse.

Prep + hob time:
20 minutes
Makes: 500ml (17fl oz)

250ml (8½fl oz) double cream
250ml (8½fl oz) whole milk
3 egg yolks
40g (1½oz) caster sugar
1 tsp vanilla bean paste
10g (¼oz) cornflour

RICH CUSTARD

1. Warm the cream and milk together in a heavy-bottomed saucepan over a medium heat until steaming but not simmering.

2. Meanwhile, whisk the egg yolks, sugar and vanilla together in a mixing bowl until pale, then add the cornflour and whisk to a paste.

3. Pour the warmed cream and milk into the bowl with the egg mixture, whisking as you go, then pour the mixture back into the pan and continue to whisk over a medium-high heat for 5-10 minutes until thickened.

Prep + hob time:
20 minutes
Makes: 500ml (17fl oz)

100ml (3½fl oz) Baileys (or other Irish cream liqueur)
400ml (13½fl oz) whole milk
3 egg yolks
40g (1½oz) caster sugar
10g (¼oz) cornflour

BAILEYS CUSTARD

1. Warm the Baileys and milk together in a heavy-bottomed saucepan over a medium heat until steaming but not simmering.

2. Meanwhile, whisk the egg yolks and sugar together in a mixing bowl until pale, then add the cornflour and whisk to a paste.

3. Pour the warmed cream and milk into the bowl with the egg mixture, whisking as you go, then pour the mixture back into the pan and continue to whisk over a medium-high heat for 5–10 minutes until thickened.

Sauces + Drizzles

Prep + hob time:
20 minutes
Makes: 500ml (17fl oz)

250ml (8½fl oz) whole milk
250ml (8½fl oz) double cream
2 vanilla chai teabags
3 egg yolks
40g (1½oz) caster sugar
10g (¼oz) cornflour

CHAI LATTE CUSTARD

1. Pour the cream and milk into a heavy-bottomed saucepan, add the teabags and warm over a medium heat until steaming but not simmering. Remove the teabags after about 5 minutes, squeezing all the cream out.

2. Meanwhile, whisk the egg yolks and sugar together in a large bowl until pale, then add the cornflour and whisk to a paste.

3. Pour the infused cream and milk into the bowl with the egg mixture, whisking as you go, then pour the mixture back into the pan and continue to whisk over a medium-high heat for 5–10 minutes until thickened.

GEORGE LOVES A TIP!

— Pouring the milk and cream into the egg mixture helps to temper the eggs so you don't end up with scrambled eggs in your custard!

— If you really want to make your custard pop, use milk with a higher fat percentage than whole milk, such as Jersey Gold, for an even richer, creamier taste.

CHOCOLATE FUDGE SAUCE

Prep + hob time:
15 minutes
Makes: 1.1kg (2lb 7oz)

This is a viscous, rich, stickathickalicious, sweet sauce you can use to drizzle over desserts, flavour buttercreams, layer-up cakes, ladle into your mouth… It's perfect poured over the Espresso Martini Hot Fudge Brownie Sundae on page 179.

250g (9oz) caster sugar
150g (5¼oz) light brown sugar
75g (2¾oz) cocoa powder
50g (2oz) plain flour
400g (14oz) condensed milk
75g (2¾oz) butter
150ml (5¼fl oz) water
½ tsp vanilla bean paste

1. This one's as simple as can be. Just pour, dump and chuck all your ingredients into a large, deep saucepan over a low heat.

2. Stir occasionally until the sugars begin to dissolve and the butter starts to melt, then crank the heat up to high and allow to simmer away for 10 minutes until reduced and thick.

3. Turn off the heat and leave to cool, and marvel as it thickens up some more.

GEORGE LOVES A TIP!

— You can easily halve this recipe, though how irritating to only use half a tin of condensed milk?! Alternatively, you can store any leftover sauce in the fridge for up to two weeks.

EASY LIKE SUNDAY MORNING

I'm a bit of a workaholic (seven days a week, minimum 12 hours a day and the hypertension to prove it), but I'm told that there are people who take days off and just bake for fun?! Wild concept, if you ask me, although that's probably what you're all doing, so these recipes are for those slower days when you want to make something a little simpler and lounge about as you go.

While recipe testing for this book I've been listening to relaxing ambient music inspired by the film *Dune*. I can't stand the radio because who wants to listen to other people's dry conversations between songs you don't know, don't like and didn't pick?! I may have spent a Sunday morning up at the bakery disassociating to Paul and Chani's love theme while eating an entire tray of Pumpkin Spice + Caramelized White Chocolate Cookies (see page 44) – they're even more incredible with Thiccc Caramel (see page 22) sandwiched between them.

I've also slipped a few breakfast-esque bakes into this chapter – not because they didn't fit into any of the other chapters (so cynical of you!) but because if you're going to be baking lazily at any time of day, it'll most likely be morning, so might as well have a couple of recipes you can indulge in by mid-morning. Although don't let that stop you baking and eating a slice of Piña Colada Pie (see page 105) at 6am!

Chocolate Rocky Road Tower	37
Millionaire's Shortbread	38
Ultimate Blondies	39
Strawberry Milkshake Cookies	40
Oat + Choc Chip Cookies	41
Pumpkin Spice + Caramelized White Chocolate Cookies	44
Seashell Brownies	47
Peanut Butter Crispy Clusters	48
Galaxy Caramel Lump	51
Biscoff Blondies	52
Pumpkin Spice Cake	55
Chocolate Cookie Dough	56
Almond Croissant Loaf Cake	59
Cookie Cereal	60

CHOCOLATE ROCKY ROAD TOWER

Prep time:
1½ hours plus chilling
Serves: 16

Rocky road can only be improved with a layer of nougat, and you won't convince me otherwise! These bars are rich, but that just means they'll go a long way and the nougat, so long as you've whisked it enough, will hold its shape and store for up to a week in an airtight container in the fridge.

For the rocky road:
500g (18oz) milk chocolate, broken into pieces
75g (2¾oz) butter
200g (7oz) chocolate spread
75g (2¾oz) mini marshmallows
200g (7oz) digestive biscuits, crumbled
100g (3½oz) Milky Way bars, chopped
100g (3½oz) Mars bars, chopped

For the nougat:
250g (9oz) caster sugar
150g (5¼oz) honey
22g (¾oz) liquid glucose
125ml (4¼fl oz) water
2 egg whites (approx. 80g/3oz)

For the topping:
200g (7oz) milk chocolate, broken into pieces
600g (1lb 5oz) chocolate spread

1. Grease and line a 25cm (10in) square cake tin.
2. To make the rocky road, melt the chocolate and butter together in a bowl over a bain-marie, stirring until smooth.
3. Melt the chocolate spread in a small saucepan over a low heat, then add to the melted chocolate and butter. Stir to combine and set aside to cool slightly.
4. Tip the marshmallows, digestive biscuits, Milky Way bars and Mars bars into a mixing bowl and toss to combine. Pour the melted chocolate mixture over the rocky road 'rubble' and toss until well coated. Tip the mixture into the lined tin and level the surface, then refrigerate for 2 hours.
5. To make the nougat, heat the sugar, honey, liquid glucose and water in a saucepan over a medium heat, stirring occasionally, until the sugar has dissolved and formed a syrup. Turn the heat to high and bring the syrup to the boil – you want it to eventually reach 160°C (320°F).
6. When the syrup reaches 145°C (300°F) – this will take 4–5 minutes – whisk the egg whites to soft peaks with the whisk on a medium speed.
7. When the syrup reaches 160°C (320°F), slowly pour the syrup into the egg whites while whisking on a high speed. Continue to whisk for 3–5 minutes until the nougat is thickened and slightly cooled.
8. Spread the nougat over the chilled rocky road evenly, smoothing with a palette knife.
9. To make the topping, melt the chocolate in a bowl over a bain-marie, stirring until smooth. Melt the chocolate spread in a small saucepan over a low heat. Pour the melted chocolate into the melted chocolate spread, stir and set aside to cool.
10. Pour the topping over the nougat and refrigerate for at least 3 hours before slicing and serving.

GEORGE LOVES A TIP!
— Don't be tempted to skimp and use cooking chocolate, although a supermarket own brand will be just as nice as your favourite bar.

MILLIONAIRE'S SHORTBREAD

Prep + baking time:
1 hour, plus chilling
Serves: 12

This is the ultimate weekend bake and the tastiest way to use up any leftover Thiccc Caramel (see page 22).

For the shortbread base:
200g (7oz) butter
200g (7oz) plain flour
50g (2oz) wholemeal flour
50g (2oz) caster sugar
½ tsp salt flakes

For the caramel layer:
500g (1lb 2oz) Thiccc Caramel (see page 22)

For the topping:
200g (7oz) plain chocolate, broken into pieces
50g (2oz) butter

1. Preheat the oven to 160°C/140°C fan/320°F/Gas 3.

2. To make the shortbread base, rub the butter into both flours until the mixture resembles fine breadcrumbs. Add the sugar and salt and use your hands to bring the mixture together to form a dough, then press the dough into a 20cm (8in) square tin. Bake for 25 minutes until lightly golden on top, the set aside to cool.

3. Meanwhile, make the Thiccc Caramel following the method on page 22, then use it to cover the cooled shortbread evenly.

4. To make the topping, melt the chocolate and butter together in a bowl over a bain-marie, stirring until smooth. Pour the melted chocolate mixture evenly over the caramel layer and refrigerate for at least 2 hours before slicing and serving.

GEORGE LOVES A TIP!

— The trick to creating the crumbliest shortbread base is to rub the butter into the flour slowly, using the tips of your fingers, until there are no lumps left.

— If you like a milkier chocolate topping, use 200g (7oz) milk chocolate in place of the dark chocolate and reduce the butter to 40g (1½oz).

— I like adding crushed-up Maltesers to the topping for a crispy, malty bite!

ULTIMATE BLONDIES

It wasn't until after I'd finished writing *Rebel Bakes* that I perfected the blondie recipe we now use at the bakery. In fact, this one is even easier – you don't need to whisk the eggs and sugar first, just be sure to make the batter while the white chocolate and butter mixture is still warm to ensure it's silky-smooth. There are two secrets: the first is the length of time your blondie needs to set. With brownies, you can get away with a shorter time in the fridge once baked (although I always recommend at least six hours) but with blondies, it's best to leave them overnight to get that fudgy texture. The second is the cooking time. It's so hard to tell if they're cooked just by looking at them (and even by wobbling the tray) so just trust the process!

Prep + baking time:
1 hour plus chilling
Serves: 12

200g (7oz) white chocolate, broken into pieces
250g (9oz) butter
300g (10½oz) caster sugar
290g (10¼oz) plain flour
4 eggs
2 tsp vanilla bean paste
200g (7oz) white chocolate chips

1. Preheat the oven to 180°C/160°C fan/350°F/Gas 4. Grease and line a 25cm (10in) square cake tin.

2. Melt the white chocolate and butter together in a bowl over a bain-marie, stirring until smooth, then add the sugar, flour, eggs and vanilla and beat to form a smooth batter.

3. Add the white chocolate chips and stir through, then pour the mixture into the lined tin and bake for 30–35 minutes.

4. Allow the tin to cool at room temperature for about 15 minutes then refrigerate for at least 8 hours before slicing and enjoying.

GEORGE LOVES A TIP!

— The blondies will be perfectly cooked when a thermometer placed into the centre of the tray reads 103°C (217°F).

STRAWBERRY MILKSHAKE COOKIES

On a recent holiday to Orlando we ate doughnuts every single day for breakfast, and I was always arguing with my eight-year-old niece for a strawberry glazed one (obviously, I always won and it was character building for her to understand that tears don't always result in getting what you want). So as soon as I was home I decided I needed to make a strawberry bake that tasted just as good – but didn't feel quite as sinful or as much of a faff to make – as a doughnut. I settled on these cookies, and they taste just as good.

Prep + baking time:
45 minutes
Serves:
10

For the cookies:
150g (5¼oz) caster sugar
50g (2oz) light brown sugar
150g (5¼oz) butter, melted
1 egg plus 1 yolk
200g (7oz) plain flour
50g (2oz) strawberry milkshake powder
25g (1oz) milk powder
¼ tsp bicarbonate of soda
½ tsp baking powder
200g (7oz) white chocolate chips

For the strawberry glaze:
200g (7oz) strawberries, sliced
250g (9oz) icing sugar

To decorate:
Sprinkles or white chocolate curls

1. Preheat the oven to 190°C/170°C fan/375°F/Gas 5 and line three large baking trays with baking parchment.

2. Combine the sugars in a mixing bowl then pour over the melted butter. Stir until the sugars dissolve then add the whole egg and egg yolk, flour, milkshake powder, milk powder, bicarbonate of soda and baking powder. Stir well to form a dough, then add the white chocolate chips and mix to incorporate.

3. Weigh the dough and divide it into ten equal portions. Roll each portion into a ball and distribute between the lined baking trays. Bake for 10–12 minutes until starting to brown on top, then leave to cool.

4. When your cookies have cooled, make your strawberry glaze. Push the strawberries through a sieve over a measuring jug until you have 100ml (3½fl oz) of juice. Add the icing sugar to the juice and stir until smooth and fairly thick.

5. Pour a little glaze onto each cooled cookie and decorate with sprinkles and/or chocolate curls.

GEORGE LOVES A TIP!

— Sadly, due to the fresh strawberry juice in the glaze, these cookies don't last too long without becoming soggy. You can always store the glaze in the fridge and bring it back to room temperature before coating the cookies and serving if you want to make them in advance, though.

OAT + CHOC CHIP COOKIES

Prep + baking time:
30 minutes
Serves: 10–12

I'll admit that if you'd told me a couple of years ago that I would find this recipe superior to The OG Cookie in *Rebel Bakes*, I'd be flummoxed, flabbergasted and freaked out, but here we are. These are somewhere between a thiccc cookie, with their soft doughy texture, and a crisper cookie with a little crunch to the edges. Don't be tempted to skip the browning of the butter and honey – it's what gives this batch of beauties their delicious rich flavour.

150g (5¼oz) light brown sugar
50g (2oz) caster sugar
165g (5¾oz) butter
25g (1oz) honey
200g (7oz) plain flour
75g (2¾oz) oats
½ tsp baking powder
1 tsp vanilla bean paste
1 tsp salt flakes
3 egg yolks
¼ tsp bicarbonate of soda
100g (3½oz) milk chocolate chips
100g (3½oz) dark chocolate, chopped

1. Preheat the oven to 190°C/170°C fan/375°F/Gas 5 and line two large baking sheets.
2. Combine the sugars in a large mixing bowl and set aside.
3. Melt the butter and honey together in a saucepan over a medium-high heat for 3–5 minutes until the mixture starts to froth and the butter has begun to brown.
4. Pour the hot browned butter mixture into the bowl with the sugar and stir until the sugar has dissolved.
5. Add the flour, oats, baking powder, vanilla, salt, egg yolks and bicarbonate of soda and beat to form a wet but cohesive dough.
6. Add the chocolate chips and dark chocolate and mix until evenly distributed.
7. Use a scoop to dollop about 11 balls of the mixture onto the lined baking sheets and bake for 12 minutes until the edges are starting to go golden. Leave to cool before tucking in.

GEORGE LOVES A TIP!

— Browning the honey with the butter helps to intensify the flavour and is a good way of making a cheap honey taste like an expensive one.

PUMPKIN SPICE + CARAMELIZED WHITE CHOCOLATE COOKIES

These were a revelation to me because I don't usually like pumpkin spiced cookies, but having made my own spice mix, using actual pumpkin, I've been won over. These are my new favourite bake of the year – and using actual pumpkin you sure as hell know it's counting towards my five-a-day fantasy. And yes, I'm just being my usual snooty self with the title of this one… Caramelized white chocolate is, of course, its own thing (and you can make it by cooking white chocolate with a specific cocoa percentage in the oven for a specific amount of time), buuuuuuuut they make it now and call it golden or blonde chocolate, so, easier just to buy some of that tbh.

Prep + baking time: 20 minutes
Serves: 9

100g (3½oz) butter
50g (2oz) pumpkin purée
50g (2oz) caster sugar
150g (5¼oz) light brown sugar
225g (8oz) plain flour
2 egg yolks
½ tsp baking powder
¼ tsp bicarbonate of soda
½ tsp salt flakes
1 tsp ground cinnamon
¾ tsp ground ginger
½ tsp ground cloves
¼ tsp ground nutmeg
150g (5¼oz) golden/blonde white chocolate or Caramilk, chopped into chunks

1. Preheat the oven to 190°C/170°C fan/375°F/Gas 5 and line two large baking sheets.

2. Cream the butter, pumpkin purée and both sugars together until light orange and fluffy.

3. Add the flour, egg yolks, baking powder, bicarbonate of soda, salt and spices and mix to form a dough. Add the chocolate and mix to incorporate.

4. Using spoons or a scoop, dollop nine balls of dough approximately 6cm (2½in) in diameter onto the lined baking sheets, spaced well apart. Bake for 12 minutes until golden on top.

GEORGE LOVES A TIP!

— Pumpkin purée is widely available in tins in the baking or world food aisles in most supermarkets but, failing that, you can get it online for a reasonable price.

— 'Caramelized white chocolate' – baby gorgeous, I use Caramilk.

SEASHELL BROWNIES

There's something about the swirled, intertwined, merged ganache that makes me wanna eat an entire tray of these! One of the most popular items on our market stalls, the seashell chocolates are (in my opinion) a really simple way to elevate a regular brownie and makes them look extra special for a gift (even if it's just a gift to yourself). Also, I'm calling these seashell chocolates, but we all know what I mean!

Prep + baking time:
1 hour plus chilling
Serves: 12

For the brownies:
200g (7oz) dark chocolate, broken into pieces
250g (9oz) butter
300g (10½oz) golden caster sugar
4 eggs
65g (2½oz) plain flour
80g (3oz) cocoa powder
1 tsp salt
100g (3½oz) Nutella

For the ganache:
250g (9oz) milk chocolate, broken into pieces
250g (9oz) white chocolate, broken into pieces
300ml (10fl oz) double cream

To decorate:
250g (9oz) seashell chocolates

1. Preheat the oven to 180°C/160°C fan/350°F/Gas 4. Grease and line a 25cm (10in) square cake tin.
2. Melt the dark chocolate and butter together in a bowl over a bain-marie, stirring until smooth, then leave to cool.
3. Meanwhile, whisk the sugar and eggs together for 3–5 minutes until thick, pale and doubled in size.
4. Pour the cooled chocolate mixture into the egg mixture and whisk to incorporate. Sieve in the flour and cocoa powder, sprinkle with the salt and gently fold to create a smooth, shiny batter.
5. Pour into the lined tin and swirl in the nutella. Bake for 22–26 minutes until there's just a slight wobble on top, or when a thermometer reads 89°C (192°F). Leave to cool for 10 minutes at room temperature before refrigerating for at least 4 hours, preferably overnight, then remove the tin from the fridge and slice into twelve squares.
6. To make the ganache, melt the milk and white chocolate in separate bowls over bain-maries, stirring until smooth.
7. Pour 150ml (5¼fl oz) of the cream into each bowl of melted chocolate, beat until smooth and glossy then leave to thicken slightly.
8. Place alternate dollops of each ganache into a piping bag fitted with your nozzle of choice – this will create a perfect swirly effect – then pipe the ganache onto each brownie in a design of your choice and top each one with a seashell chocolate.

GEORGE LOVES A TIP!
— I like my brownies to be as fudgy as possible, so I store them in the fridge where they'll last at least a week. You can also store them in an airtight container in a cool, dry place, but as they've ganache atop, they'll only last for a couple of days.

PEANUT BUTTER CRISPY CLUSTERS

Prep time:
30 minutes, plus chilling
Serves: 14

Peanut butter is the ultimate sweet and salty sensation. These clusters, inspired by energy bites (I guess they're a pre-workout?), swing from sweet and chocolatey to salty and crispy. They're the perfect snack.

100g (3½oz) butter
150g (5¼oz) golden syrup
75g (2¾oz) crunchy or smooth peanut butter
300g (10½oz) mini marshmallows
165g (5¾oz) Reese's cereal
75g (2¾oz) pretzels or salted crisps, crushed
50g (2oz) roasted, salted peanuts
90g (3¼oz) Reese's Pieces, chilled
2 tsp vegetable oil

1. Line two large baking trays with parchment paper.

2. Heat the butter in a deep, heavy-bottomed saucepan over a medium heat for 3–5 minutes until frothy and beginning to brown.

3. Reduce the heat to low, add the golden syrup, peanut butter and marshmallows and continue to heat, stirring occasionally, until melted and combined – it will take a little while for the marshmallows to start melting but it'll be fast when they do!

4. Meanwhile combine the cereal, pretzels or salted crisps and peanuts together in a mixing bowl.

5. Tip the mallow mixture into the mixing bowl of deliciousness and stir to combine. Allow to cool for about 5 minutes until cool enough to handle then fold in the chilled Reese's Pieces to incorporate.

6. Lightly oil your hands with the vegetable oil and roll the mallow mixture into 14 golf ball-sized clusters. Place the clusters on the lined baking trays and refrigerate for an hour, then transfer to an airtight container and store in the fridge for up to five days.

GEORGE LOVES A TIP!

— You can use smooth or crunchy peanut butter in this recipe – whichever is your favourite.

— Oiling your hands with vegetable oil (or any other flavourless oil) helps to stop the mallow mixture sticking to your hands when rolling it into clusters.

Easy Like Sunday Morning

GALAXY CARAMEL LUMP

Prep time
1½ hours plus chilling
Serves: 12

Rocky road meets millionaire's shortbread in this no-bake cake that is a firm favourite at the bakery. It's great to make ahead and can also be sliced into small finger portions.

For the base:
250g (9oz) Galaxy chocolate, broken into pieces
250g (9oz) milk chocolate, broken into pieces
75g (2¾oz) butter
200g (7oz) chocolate spread
100g (3½oz) digestive biscuits, crumbled
275g (10oz) Galaxy Caramel, chopped
750g (1lb 10oz) Thiccc Caramel (see page 22)

For the topping:
200g (7oz) Galaxy chocolate, broken into pieces
400g (14oz) chocolate spread

To decorate:
120g (4½oz) Galaxy Caramel, broken into pieces

1. Grease and line a 25cm (10in) square cake tin.
2. To make the base, melt the Galaxy chocolate, milk chocolate and butter together in a bowl over a bain-marie, stirring until smooth.
3. Melt the chocolate spread in a small saucepan over a low heat then add to the melted chocolate and butter mixture, stirring to combine.
4. Combine the digestive biscuits and Galaxy Caramel together in a large bowl. Pour the melted chocolate mixture over the 'rubble' and toss until well coated. Tip the mixture into the lined tin and leave to set for at least two hours.
5. Meanwhile, make the Thiccc Caramel following the method on page 22. Spread the Thiccc Caramel evenly over the cooled base and set aside.
6. To make the topping, melt the Galaxy chocolate and chocolate spread together in a small saucepan over a low heat, stirring until smooth. Remove from the heat and allow to cool slightly.
7. Pour the topping over the Thiccc Caramel layer and decorate with pieces of Galaxy Caramel.
8. Refrigerate for 2 hours before slicing and serving.

GEORGE LOVES A TIP!
— If you want to serve this looking its best, remove from the fridge 30 minutes before slicing so the base doesn't cause a crumbly catastrophe.

Easy Like Sunday Morning

BISCOFF BLONDIES

Biscoff spread is the greatest thing to ever come in a jar and it pairs perfectly with blondies, which need a lot of vanilla to give them their delicious taste. I like using the smooth Biscoff spread, but you can mix it up with the crunchy variation if you like. If you're feeling extra, you can even submerge a few biscuits in the batter for a bit more texture. These blondies are perfect sliced into mini pieces, stacked up with Biscoff spread for glue and drizzled with yet more Biscoff spread for an extra special birthday cake.

Prep + baking time: 1 hour, plus chilling
Serves: 12

For the blondie batter:
250g (9oz) butter
200g (7oz) white chocolate, broken into pieces
300g (10½oz) caster sugar
4 eggs
290g (10¼oz) plain flour
2 tsp vanilla bean paste
75g (2¾oz) Biscoff spread

For the Biscoff ganache:
500g (1lb 2oz) white chocolate, broken into pieces
300ml (10fl oz) double cream
50g (2oz) Biscoff spread

To decorate:
Biscoff biscuits

1. Preheat the oven to 180°C/160°C fan/350°F/Gas 4. Grease and line a 25cm (10in) square cake tin.

2. To make the batter, melt the butter and white chocolate together in a large bowl over a bain-marie, stirring until smooth, then add the sugar, eggs, flour and vanilla and beat to form a smooth batter. Pour into the lined tin.

3. Spoon the Biscoff spread into a piping bag, snip a 5mm (¼in) hole in the end and pipe zigzags over the blondie batter, then swirl the Biscoff spread through the batter using a palette knife. Bake for 30–35 minutes until golden on top.

4. Leave to cool for 15 minutes until the tin is no longer hot to the touch, then refrigerate for at least 8 hours to set.

5. When you're ready to serve, make the Biscoff ganache by melting the white chocolate in a bowl over a bain-marie, then add the cream and beat until smooth and glossy. Add the Biscoff spread and beat to incorporate.

6. Remove the blondies from the fridge and slice to your desired size. Spoon the ganache into a piping bag fitted with your favourite nozzle and pipe the ganache over the blondies, then decorate with Biscoff biscuits and serve.

GEORGE LOVES A TIP!

— You can replace the Biscoff spread with Nutella, jam or any other spread you fancy to create a delicious blondie.

— Achieving the perfect blondie texture is a fine art. The longer you leave your blondies cooling out of the fridge, the more likely they are to become cakey. But if you put the hot baking tray into the fridge before it's had the chance to cool a little, your glass fridge shelf will smash. So, 15 minutes feels like a reasonable compromise to me.

PUMPKIN SPICE CAKE

Prep + baking time:
1 hour, plus cooling
Serves: 12

I'm not a pumpkin spice latté kinda boy but it seems a lot of people are, so this is the ideal cake for autumn! It's moist and crumbly and adding cinnamon to the buttercream brings a little extra spice.

For the sponge:
250g (9oz) butter
50ml (2fl oz) vegetable oil
200g (7oz) light brown sugar
100g (3½oz) caster sugar
6 eggs
300g (10½oz) self-raising flour
½ tsp ground cinnamon
½ tsp ground ginger
¼ tsp ground nutmeg
¼ tsp ground cloves
1½ tsp baking powder
200g (7oz) pumpkin purée

For the buttercream:
300g (10½oz) butter
600g (1lb 5oz) icing sugar
½ tsp ground cinnamon

1. Preheat the oven to 180°C/160°C fan/350°F/Gas 4 and line four 20cm (8in) round cake tins.

2. To make the sponges, cream the butter, oil and sugars together until pale and fluffy. Add the eggs, flour, spices, baking powder and pumpkin purée and beat to form a batter.

3. Divide the batter between the four lined tins and bake for 18–22 minutes until a skewer comes out clean, then leave to cool.

4. To make the buttercream, beat the butter until pale and creamy then add the icing sugar and cinnamon and beat again until smooth. Use half of the buttercream to stack the sponges on top of each another, and the other half to coat the sides and top of the cake. Smooth the buttercream with a cake scraper or palette knife and decorate as you wish.

GEORGE LOVES A TIP!

— This is a really light and fluffy cake that will keep for up to five days at room temperature – just make sure to cover any exposed sponge after cutting.

— This cake can be quite crumbly to ice. Chilling it once you've stacked the cakes will allow it to firm before icing the outside.

CHOCOLATE COOKIE DOUGH

Prep time: 15 minutes
Serves: 4

Even better than regular cookie dough and, frankly, delicious spread onto cookies. Scoop it straight out of the bowl, tuck in and enjoy – the heat-treated flour and lack of egg means this is safe to eat as it is and doesn't need baking.

200g (7oz) plain flour
50g (2oz) cocoa powder
225g (8oz) butter
100g (3½oz) light brown sugar
100g (3½oz) caster sugar
1 tsp vanilla bean paste
½ tsp salt
25ml (1fl oz) whole milk
100g (3½oz) chocolate chips

1. Preheat the oven to 180°C/160°C fan/350°F/Gas 4.

2. Mix the flour and cocoa powder together in a bowl then spread out evenly onto a baking tray. Bake for 8 minutes, then leave to cool completely.

3. Meanwhile, cream the butter and sugars together for at least 3 minutes until very pale and fluffy.

4. Add the vanilla and salt to the butter and sugar mixture, then sieve in the cooled flour and cocoa powder. Mix until a dough begins to form.

5. Slowly add the milk, stirring after each addition, to form a soft dough. Add the chocolate chips and mix to combine.

GEORGE LOVES A TIP!
— Chop up your favourite chocolate and mix through the dough to really make this easy sweet treat your own!

ALMOND CROISSANT LOAF CAKE

Prep + baking time:
1¼ hours
Serves: 6–8

Guess I gotta eat my words because you can read about my disdain for almond essence on page 187 of *Rebel Bakes*, and now here I am, older, wiser and with diminished taste buds because I now can't get enough of the stuff! It's what gives this loaf cake real zing. This delicious breakfast-style bake, with its fluffy centre and crisp topping, can be enjoyed hot or cold.

For the sponge:
200g (7oz) butter
125g (4½oz) caster sugar
75g (2¾oz) light brown sugar
4 eggs, beaten
150g (5¼oz) self-raising flour
50g (2oz) ground almonds

For the frangipane filling:
75g (2¾oz) butter
75g (2¾oz) caster sugar
1 egg
75g (2¾oz) ground almonds
½ tsp almond extract

For the topping:
160g (5½oz) ready-to-bake croissant dough (approximately 3 croissants)
2 tbsp demerara sugar

1. Preheat the oven to 180°C/160°C fan/350°F/Gas 4. Grease and line a 900g (2lb) loaf tin.

2. To make the sponge, cream the butter and sugars together until light and fluffy. Slowly add the eggs with the mixer on low speed and mix until fully incorporated. Add the flour and ground almonds and beat to a smooth batter. Set aside.

3. To make the frangipane filling, cream the butter and sugar together until light and fluffy. Add the egg, ground almonds and almond extract and beat to a smooth paste.

4. Spoon half of the sponge batter into the lined loaf tin followed by the frangipane filling, then top with the remaining batter.

5. Unfurl the croissant dough and slice into triangles (you may also need some larger squares of dough to cover the centre of the loaf cake), then layer the dough triangles over the batter, overlapping as needed to cover.

6. Sprinkle over the demerara sugar and bake for 50 minutes, then increase the oven temperature to 180°C/160°C fan/350°F/Gas 4 and bake for a further 10 minutes. Leave to cool.

GEORGE LOVES A TIP!

— To make this loaf cake last as long as possible, place in an airtight container and store in a cool, dry place for up to three days.

— Not saying I've done this, but a couple of day-old slices make an amazing French toast.

COOKIE CEREAL

Do you ever go through a phase of eating nothing but cereal for a couple of weeks and then don't go near it again for six months or so? Well, that's what happens to me at least twice a year and cereal doesn't get better than these mini cookies – when soaked in milk they create a milkshake to slurp up at the bottom of your bowl. You can customize the recipe as you wish (dark or white chocolate, add some mini meringues, chuck in a bit of cinnamon…) but I love it just as it is. A simple treat. If you warm a bowlful before pouring over your milk, you'll be in absolute comfort heaven!

Prep + baking time: 30 minutes
Serves: 2

125g (4½oz) butter
50g (2oz) brown sugar
25g (1oz) caster sugar
1 egg
150g (5¼oz) plain flour
½ tsp salt
50g (2oz) milk chocolate, very finely chopped
¼ tsp vanilla bean paste

1. Preheat the oven to 180°C/160°C fan/350°F/Gas 4 and line three large baking sheets.

2. Cream the butter and sugars together until light and fluffy then add the egg, flour and salt and mix to form a dough. Make sure that your chocolate is very finely chopped (and I mean very finely – it's got to fit through the hole in a piping bag!) and mix into the dough.

3. Spoon the dough into a piping bag and cut off the end to form a hole about 5mm (¼in) wide. Pipe around 100 small blobs of the dough onto the lined baking sheets, leaving enough space for the cookies to expand as they bake. Bake for 5 minutes until the edges of the cookies are starting to turn golden.

4. Leave to cool before transferring to an airtight container and storing at room temperature for up to one week.

GEORGE LOVES A TIP!

— You could roll the dough into cookie shapes using your hands but it takes ages, so I really do recommend piping them if you have a piping bag handy.

— Remember that the cookies won't need long in the oven due to their size, so don't be tempted to leave them in for any longer!

BAKING TO SHARE

The greedy capitalist in me interprets this chapter as 'baking for money' because these are the best bakes to slice up and sell, sell, sell! However, it's really lots of favourites from the bakery and the most requested recipes from my social media. Reluctantly (and after MUCH pestering from some of you), I'm giving you the secrets to our sharing recipes and they slot in here perfectly.

Most of these bakes stand out from the rest of the book in another way; they're not comfort bakes in the sense that you're tucked up on the sofa with a blanket, but more that they're based around happy memories. Lots of spring and summer celebrations need comfort bakes, too, and these are just the festive fit!

I was channelling school fetes, charity bake sales and finding ways of letting your colleagues know you're better than them with this lot, but they're great to share with friends, too!

Salted Caramel Cornflake Rocky Road	66
Milkybar + Mini Egg Cookie Millionaires	69
Nutella Brownies	70
Churros Blondies	73
Earl Grey + Lavender Cake	74
Blondie Roll	77
Raspberry Ripple Cheesecake Sandwiches	78
Raspberry + Lemon Cheesecake Blondies	80
Triple Chocolate Cornflake Roll	83
Peaches + Cream Stuffed Thiccc Cookies	84
Pistachio Cookie Millionaires	87

SALTED CARAMEL CORNFLAKE ROCKY ROAD

I know what you're thinking... I don't know when to stop. You're completely right, but it's what results in these magical moments! Creating a slightly thinner layer of both rocky road and the salted caramellow cornflake mixture means that this is still manageable to pick up and eat, while not being too sickly. I like using caramel chocolate for the base to pair with the sticky, crunchy topping, but it'll work with different chocolates, too.

Prep time:
1 hour, plus chilling
Serves: 12

For the caramel cornflake topping:
450g (1lb) Salted Caramel (see page 23)
50g (2oz) mini marshmallows
100g (3½oz) milk chocolate, broken into pieces
350g (12¼oz) cornflakes

For the rocky road:
300g (10½oz) milk chocolate, broken into pieces
40g (1½oz) butter
125g (4½oz) chocolate spread
75g (2¾oz) mini marshmallows
75g (2¾oz) chocolate caramel wafers, chopped
50g (2oz) Rolos, chopped
40g (1½oz) Munchies, chopped
50g (2oz) caramel chocolate bars, broken into pieces

1. Grease and line a 25cm (10in) square cake tin.
2. To make the topping, heat the salted caramel, marshmallows and chocolate together in a large saucepan over a low heat, stirring occasionally, until the marshmallows have almost melted.
3. Remove from the heat and beat until the marshmallows have completely dissolved and the mixture has increased in volume.
4. Add half of the cornflakes and stir to coat in the caramel mixture, then add the remaining cornflakes and continue to stir until completely coated in the caramallow concoction. Set aside to cool slightly.
5. To make the rocky road, melt the chocolate and butter together in a bowl over a bain-marie. Melt the chocolate spread in a small saucepan over a low heat then add to the chocolate and butter mixture and fold through.
6. Tip the marshmallows, caramel wafers, Rolos, Munchies and caramel chocolate into a large bowl and toss to combine.
7. Pour the melted chocolate mixture into the bowl and stir everything together. Decant the rocky road into the lined tin and shake to level out. Allow to stand for 25 minutes to set slightly.
8. Tip the cornflake mixture over the rocky road and very gently spread it out evenly to cover. Cover with cling film and refrigerate for at least 4 hours before slicing.

GEORGE LOVES A TIP!

— The timings for adhering the cornflakes to the rocky road base are crucial to stop the cornflakes from soaking up too much of the caramellow mixture and becoming soggy. As soon as the rocky road has been standing for 25 minutes, spread the cornflake mixture on top.

— This bake is best stored in an airtight container in the fridge for up to five days.

MILKYBAR + MINI EGG COOKIE MILLIONAIRES

When thinking of comfort bakes, most people think of the colder winter months, but making these millionaires marks the beginning of Easter for me. They are one of the most popular items we sell at markets and they're pretty simple to make. Swapping out the traditional shortbread base for a cookie one ups the mini egg dosage (who doesn't love a mini egg?) and makes these even more indulgent.

Prep + baking time: 1½ hours
Serves: 20

For the cookie base:
150g (5¼oz) butter
120g (4½oz) light brown sugar
80g (3oz) caster sugar
2 egg yolks
225g (8oz) plain flour
½ tsp baking powder
¼ tsp bicarbonate of soda
½ tsp salt flakes
200g (7oz) chocolate Mini Eggs

For the caramel layer:
500g (1lb) Thiccc Caramel (see page 22)

For the ganache:
200g (7oz) Milkybar
100ml (3½fl oz) double cream

For decorating:
150g (5¼oz) chocolate Mini Eggs

1. Preheat the oven to 190°C/170°C fan/375°F/Gas 5. Grease and line a 20cm (8in) square cake tin.

2. To make the cookie base, cream the butter and sugars together until light and fluffy. Add the egg yolks, flour, baking powder, bicarbonate of soda and salt and mix to form a dough.

3. Add the Mini Eggs and mix to incorporate, then press the dough into the lined tin. Bake for 13–15 minutes until golden on top, then leave to cool.

4. Meanwhile, make the Thiccc Caramel following the method on page 22, then spread the caramel evenly over the cooled cookie base.

5. To make the ganache, melt the Milkybar in a bowl over a bain-marie, stirring until smooth, then leave to cool for 1 minute. Add the cream and stir until glossy and smooth.

6. Pour the melted Milkybar ganache over the caramel and decorate with the Mini Eggs. Pop in the fridge to set for at least 2 hours before slicing and serving.

GEORGE LOVES TIP!
— I've gone with Mini Eggs here because they're surely the most popular of the Easter chocolates. However, you can play about and use whichever Easter treats you love most.

NUTELLA BROWNIES

Not to get in trouble with a certain – dare I say, iconic – 1* star reviewer of my last book *Rebel Bakes* again, but I do love a bulge and this is a favourite of mine. She who shall not be named even had an issue with the fact that a pornstar martini is called a pornstar martini (I googled it and her real beef is with a man named Douglas who created the drink). However, further reading did reveal that the origins of the name trace back to a strip club in South Africa, so the debauchery does linger somewhere. Take from that what you will...

Prep + baking time:
2 hours, plus chilling
Serves: 16

For the brownie base:
250g (9oz) butter
200g (7oz) dark chocolate, broken into pieces
250g (9oz) golden caster sugar
4 eggs
65g (2½oz) plain flour
80g (3oz) cocoa powder
1 tsp salt
100g (3½oz) Nutella

For the caramel layer:
750g (1lb 10oz) Thiccc Caramel (see page 22)
150g (5¼oz) Nutella

For the chocolate layer:
400g (14oz) milk chocolate, broken into pieces
800g (1lb 12oz) Nutella
150g (5¼oz) Hobnob biscuits
16 Ferrero Rochers

1. Preheat the oven to 180°C/160°C fan/350°F/Gas 4. Grease and line a deep 25cm (10in) square cake tin.

2. To make the brownie base, melt the butter and dark chocolate together in a bowl over a bain-marie, stirring until smooth. Set aside to cool slightly.

3. Meanwhile, whisk the sugar and eggs together for 3–5 minutes until thick, pale and fluffy, then pour in the melted chocolate mixture and whisk again until incorporated.

4. Sieve the flour and cocoa powder into the bowl, sprinkle with the salt and fold until smooth, then pour into the lined tin.

5. Warm the Nutella in a small saucepan over a low heat until thinned, then pour into a piping bag and pipe Nutella swirls in to the brownie batter.

6. Bake for 22–26 minutes until there's just a slight wobble on top, or when a thermometer reads 89°C (192°F). Leave to cool for 10 minutes at room temperature, then refrigerate for at least 2 hours to firm up.

7. Meanwhile make the Thiccc Caramel following the method on page 22 then mix with the Nutella until smooth and well combined.

8. Spread the Nutella and caramel mixture onto the chilled brownie base and smush it into the corners to create an even layer.

9. To make the chocolate layer, melt the chocolate and Nutella together in a small saucepan over a low heat, stirring until smooth. Pour half of the chocolate mixture over the caramel layer. Top with the whole Hobnobs and refrigerate for around an hour or until set.

10. Top with the remaining chocolate mixture (you may have to warm it through again), decorate with the Ferrero Rochers and refrigerate for at least 6 hours before slicing up and serving.

GEORGE LOVES A TIP!

— Use the deepest tin you can for this, as all of the layers result in a tall bake.

— Furthermore, the tall bake means you can easily slice this into many pieces. I've said it serves 16 because I don't want to sound greedy, but if you crumble the Ferrero Rochers on top rather than using them whole to portion the brownie into 16, you could get double the number of servings out of your tray.

CHURROS BLONDIES

Let's be real here, churros, especially those from street-food vendors these days, are perennially disappointing. I reckon a lot of this has to do with their frying, therefore, let's just cut that bit out and focus on the delicious flavours!

Everyone has a different spice tolerance, but, if you think you can handle the heat, serve alongside a spicy chocolate dipping sauce!

Prep + baking time:
1 hour plus chilling
Serves: 12

250g (9oz) butter
200g (7oz) white chocolate
225g (8oz) caster sugar
4 eggs
290g (10¼oz) plain flour
2 tsp vanilla bean paste
1 tbsp cinnamon
200g (7oz) icing sugar
75ml (2½fl oz) water
75g (2¾oz) caster sugar
1 tbsp cinnamon
50g (2oz) chilli chocolate

1. Preheat the oven to 180°C/160°C fan/350°F/Gas 4. Grease and line a 25cm (10in) square cake tin.

2. Melt the butter and white chocolate together in a bowl over a bain-marie, stirring until smooth. Beat in the sugar, eggs, flour, tablespoon of cinnamon and vanilla bean paste until you form a smooth batter.

3. Next, pour into the lined tin and bake for 30-35 minutes until golden on top.

4. Allow the tin to cool at room temperature for about 15 minutes while you make your topping.

5. Mix the icing sugar and water together and stir until smooth. Pour over the cooled blondie, spreading to evenly coat it all.

6. In a separate bowl, combine your caster sugar and cinnamon together before sprinkling over the top. Refrigerate for at least 8 hours to set.

7. Once set, melt the chilli chocolate and drizzle all over the blondie to decorate.

GEORGE LOVES A TIP!

— Pouring the glaze onto these churros blondies helps give an adhesion for the cinnamon sugar to stick to. The sugar content is no higher, as it would otherwise be in the blondies themselves.

EARL GREY + LAVENDER CAKE

This combination of flavours may sound overpowering, or like it'll just taste of the smell of lavender, but it's actually harmonious, well balanced and one of my favourite summer flavour combos. I like lady grey tea but the flavour isn't quite strong enough to come through in a cake, so earl grey is perfect and easier to get hold of. Although there isn't much milk to be infused by the tea, it will go a long way in strength and the flavour will come out even more when baked.

Prep + baking time:
1 hour plus cooling
Serves: 12

For the sponge:
75ml (2½fl oz) whole milk
4 earl grey teabags
300g (10½oz) butter
300g (10½oz) caster sugar
6 eggs
300g (10½oz) self-raising flour
1½ tsp baking powder

For the buttercream:
300g (10½oz) butter
600g (1lb 5oz) icing sugar
½ tsp lavender extract
Purple food colouring, as desired

1. Preheat the oven to 180°C/160°C fan/350°F/Gas 4. Grease and line three 20cm (8in) round cake tins.

2. To make the sponge, pour the milk into a small saucepan over a low heat, add the teabags and heat for 5 minutes until steaming. Remove from the heat and set aside to steep further while the milk cools to room temperature.

3. Cream the butter and sugar together until light and fluffy then add the eggs, flour and baking powder and beat to form a smooth batter.

4. Squeeze the milk from the teabags, being careful not to split the bags, before discarding. Pour the infused milk into the batter and fold through to form a deliciously scented batter that's light brown in colour.

5. Divide the batter equally between the three lined tins and bake for 18–22 minutes until a skewer comes out clean, then allow to cool.

6. To make the buttercream, beat the butter until pale and creamy then add the icing sugar and beat again until smooth. Add the lavender extract and purple food colouring as desired and mix to incorporate.

7. To assemble, level the tops of the sponges using a serrated knife and cover the top of one of the sponges with around a quarter of the buttercream. Layer another sponge on top and repeat, topping with the final sponge layer. Use the remaining buttercream to cover the top and sides of the cake, smoothing with a cake scraper or palette knife. Decorate as you wish – I like using edible flowers.

GEORGE LOVES A TIP!
— Look out for lavender extract instead of essence and remember that a little goes a long way!
— This cake will keep for up to five days at room temperature, as long as the exposed sponge is covered between servings.

GEORGE LOVES A TIP!

— If you're opting for the white chocolate and raspberry flavour, make a speedy ganache by heating 300g of white chocolate with 175g of double cream in the microwave in short 15 second bursts. Mix in between rounds until smooth and combined before spreading.

BLONDIE ROLL

Prep + baking time:
4 hours, plus chilling
Serves: 12

A single serving of blondie just isn't special anymore, so turning the blondie into a roll (tarting it up at Christmas as a yule log) and creating a dessert you can now slice upon serving is the new way forward.

For the blondie:
250g (9oz) butter
200g (7oz) white chocolate, broken into pieces
300g (10½oz) caster sugar
4 eggs
290g (10¼oz) plain flour
2 tsp vanilla bean paste

For the filling:
500g (1lb 2oz) Nutella or Biscoff spread or 475g (1lb 1oz) white chocolate ganache with a generous spread of raspberry jam on top

For the topping:
400g (14oz) Nutella, Biscoff or white chocolate spread
200g (7oz) milk chocolate if using Nutella or white chocolate if making Biscoff or white chocolate and raspberry
a large handful of your choice of topping, I used freeze dried raspberries, crushed Biscoff biscuits, or hazelnuts, chopped to create three separate flavours

1. Preheat the oven to 180°C/160°C fan/350°F/Gas 4. Grease and line a 25cm (10in) square cake tin.

2. Melt the butter and white chocolate together in a large bowl over a bain-marie, stirring until smooth, then set aside to cool a little.

3. Add the sugar, eggs, flour and vanilla to the melted chocolate mixture and beat to a smooth batter. Pour the batter into the lined tin and bake for 30–35 minutes until golden on top.

4. Leave to cool for 15 minutes until the tin is no longer hot to the touch, then refrigerate for at least 8 hours to set – this will give it the perfect fudgy texture.

5. Remove the blondie from the fridge and set aside to bring it back to room temperature. Meanwhile, line a 35 x 25cm (14 x 10in) baking tray with baking parchment.

6. Remove the blondie from the tin and slice away the crusts. Transfer the blondie to a large bowl, breaking it up into small pieces as you go, and then mush it with a fork.

7. Tip the crumbled blondie into the lined tin and push it down evenly with your hands to smooth. Refrigerate for 15 minutes to allow it to firm up.

8. Smother with your filling of choice – my favourites are Nutella, Biscoff or white chocolate ganache and raspberry jam – and spread to an even layer before returning to the fridge for a further 20 minutes to firm up.

9. Use the greaseproof paper to slide the blondie roll off of the baking tray and onto a work surface. Using the greaseproof to guide you, fold one of the longer ends of mixture into itself and create motion, while using the force of peeling the greaseproof away from you, to tightly roll up the filling covered blondie. Squash and smooth the edges and use your hands to rub the roll into an even girth if needed. Chill for 30 minutes.

10. Now add the topping of your choice. We've opted for milk chocolate for the Nutella version, or white chocolate for the Biscoff and white chocolate and raspberry. Melt your chosen chocolate and mix with 400g (14oz) melted Nutella, Biscoff or white chocolate spread. Mix together before pouring over the roll. Sprinkle over the hazelnuts, freeze dried raspberries or biscuit crumbs and refrigerate again for an hour before slicing up.

Baking to Share

RASPBERRY RIPPLE CHEESECAKE SANDWICHES

You've probably worked out by now that I love a creamy filling – cornflake crevices, sandwiches and of course in cakes – but these biscuits take the crown for filling-to-sandwich ratio. They are the perfect treat in summer and the rounds can be made ahead and sandwiched just before eating if you want to serve them at a party. Be sure to wrap in parchment paper or a napkin to catch any cheesecake smushing out the sides as you try and get your jaw around them!

Prep + baking time:
30 minutes, plus chilling
Serves: 6

For the biscuit rounds:
800g (1lb 12oz) digestive biscuits, crushed
450g (1lb) salted butter, melted

For the raspberry coulis:
150g (5¼oz) raspberries
Juice of 1 lemon
25g (1oz) caster sugar

For the cheesecake filling:
450g (1lb) cream cheese
225ml (7½fl oz) double cream
75g (2¾oz) icing sugar
50g (2oz) raspberries

1. To make the biscuit rounds, tip the crushed digestives into a bowl and pour over the melted butter. Toss until the biscuit crumbs are well coated in the butter, then set aside for 10 minutes.

2. Meanwhile, line a large baking sheet with parchment paper.

3. Use a burger press to create the biscuit rounds. Dollop a couple of tablespoons of the biscuit mixture into a burger press and squash down to create an even disc. Decant onto the lined baking sheet and repeat to create six rounds. Refrigerate for at least an hour.

4. To make the raspberry coulis, heat the raspberries, lemon juice and sugar in a small saucepan over a low heat for 30 minutes until reduced to a jam-like consistency. Set aside to cool.

5. To make the filling, whisk the cream cheese, cream and icing sugar together for 3–5 minutes until thick. Fold in the raspberries to create a ripple effect. Spoon the filling into a piping bag and cut a hole around 1cm (½in) in the end.

6. Remove the biscuit rounds from the fridge and pipe circles of filling close to the edges of half the biscuits, leaving half plain. Fill the centres with the raspberry coulis and top with the plain biscuit rounds. Continue with the remaining biscuit rounds then refrigerate until ready to serve.

GEORGE LOVES A TIP!

— Tipping the biscuit rounds from the burger press onto the paper can be tricky and result in a crumbly mixture flying everywhere, so don't rush!

— Store the assembled sandwiches in an airtight container in the fridge and use within a day to ensure the biscuits stay crisp and don't absorb moisture from the coulis or cheesecake filling. Alternatively, the rounds, coulis and filling can be made ahead and stored in the fridge separately then assembled just before serving.

RASPBERRY + LEMON CHEESECAKE BLONDIES

Sweet and tart are two words I use to describe myself, often, but they also apply to these blondies!

Swirling all of these flavours together helps add both new textures and flavours into the mix and is another way to take blondies to the next level!

And, as always, trust the process with blondies... they never really look cooked but too far done and they lose all their textural deliciousness.

Prep and bake time:
1 hour 20 minutes plus chilling time
Serves: 12

For the blondie:
250g (9oz) butter
200g (7oz) white chocolate, broken into pieces
1 tsp vanilla bean paste
250g (9oz) sugar
4 eggs
280g (10oz) plain flour
2 tsp cornflour

For the cheesecake:
165g (5¾oz) cream cheese
35ml (1¼fl oz) double cream
10g (¼oz) caster sugar
1 tsp cornflour
1 tsp vanilla bean paste

175g Lemon Curd (see page 25)
150g (5¼oz) fresh raspberries

1. Heat the oven to 160°C/140°C fan/320°F/Gas 3. Grease and line a 25cm (10in) square cake tin.

2. Make the blondie by melting together the butter and white chocolate, before mixing through the vanilla. Add the caster sugar, eggs, plain flour and cornflour and beat together to form a silky smooth batter.

3. Whisk together the cream cheese, double cream, caster sugar, cornflour and vanilla until thick.

4. Pour the blondie mixture into your lined tin. Place the lemon curd into a piping bag and pipe in a zigzag inside the blondie (aim for about halfway in!). Next, place the cheesecake into a piping bag and pipe in a zigzag along the top of the blondie. Use a skewer or butter knife to swirl the two together and evenly distribute the flavours across the tray. Finally, push the raspberries gently into the batter.

5. Bake for 50–55 minutes until lightly golden on top and a skewer comes out clean from the batter. Leave to cool for 10 minutes before refrigerating for at least 4 hours, preferably overnight, before slicing.

GEORGE LOVES A TIP!

— Piping the lemon curd into the blondie helps separate the layers and let each flavour stand out, as well as reducing its chances of catching on top of the blondie while baking.

— The longer you leave your blondies in the fridge, the greater the fudgy texture of them, just the same as brownies.

— These will store for up to three days in an airtight container in the fridge.

TRIPLE CHOCOLATE CORNFLAKE ROLL

Prep + baking time:
2 hours, plus chilling
Serves: 12

I've been inundated with requests for our cornflake roll recipe since they went viral online. The mixture is the same as our other cornflake delights, although the method is a little trickier to get right. Once you master it, you can adapt this recipe with lots of different flavours and even try the same technique with other bakes, too.

For the cornflake roll:
300g (10½oz) Salted Caramel (see page 23)
38g (1½oz) mini marshmallows
75g (2¾oz) milk chocolate, broken into pieces
250g (8½oz) cornflakes

For the ganache:
150g (5¼oz) milk chocolate, broken into pieces
150g (5¼oz) white chocolate, broken into pieces
150g (5¼oz) dark chocolate, broken into pieces
300ml (10½fl oz) double cream

1. Line a 36x26cm (14 x 10in) tray with parchment paper that overlaps the tray on all sides.

2. To make the cornflake roll, first prepare the Salted Caramel following the method on page 23.

3. Heat the Salted Caramel, marshmallows and chocolate together in a large saucepan over a low heat, stirring occasionally, until the marshmallows have almost melted.

4. Remove the pan from the heat and beat until the marshmallows have completely dissolved and the mixture has thickened and increased in volume.

5. Add half of the cornflakes and stir to coat in the caramel mixture. Add the remaining cornflakes and continue to stir until completely coated in the caramallow concoction. Set aside for 20 minutes to cool.

6. Tip the caramel cornflake mixture onto the lined baking tray and spread out evenly. Refrigerate for 30 minutes.

7. Meanwhile, make the ganache. Melt the milk, white and dark chocolates by microwaving in separate bowls in short bursts, stirring until smooth, then add 100ml (3½fl oz) of the cream to each bowl and stir until glossy.

8. Remove the cornflake mixture from the fridge. Spread half of the white chocolate ganache onto one third of the cornflakes lengthways, followed by half of the milk chocolate ganache onto the middle third and finally half of the dark chocolate ganache on the final third (you'll need the other half of each ganache left over for coating the outside of the roll).

9. Using the parchment paper, lift the chocolate-covered cornflake mixture out of the tray and onto your work surface. Starting at the white chocolate end, roll the cornflake mixture up as tightly as possible, squashing it together as you go, until you've created a cornflake roll!

10. Coat the outside of the roll with the remaining ganache then refrigerate for at least 1 hour until completely set.

11. Remove from the fridge, slice up and store in an airtight container in the fridge for up to five days.

Baking to Share

PEACHES + CREAM STUFFED THICCC COOKIES

Oh, how I love peaches and cream! These stuffed cookies differ from my usual in that they're stuffed after baking and the cream is dolloped on top. This way you don't need to worry about haemorrhaging peach juices and soggy cream dribbling out onto baking trays – and they taste much more like a pudding. I don't know what it is about cold cream on a warm dessert that makes it taste so much better but it's truly unrivalled! The trick here is to make the dough in advance of baking to allow the dough enough time to firm up in the fridge – this will control the spread of the cookies and ensure they provide the perfect home for those smooth, melt-in-your-mouth peaches.

Prep + baking time:
1 hour, plus overnight chilling
Serves: 5

For the cookies:
200g (7oz) butter
220g (7¾oz) light brown sugar
3 egg yolks
370g (13oz) plain flour
½ tsp baking powder
½ tsp salt
30g (1⅛oz) cornflour
1 tsp vanilla bean paste
200g (7oz) white chocolate chips

For the peach filling:
3 peaches, approx. 450g (1lb)
100g (3½oz) caster sugar
1 tsp lemon juice
200g (7oz) clotted cream

1. To make the cookies, cream the butter and sugar together until light and fluffy, then add the egg yolks, flour, baking powder, salt, cornflour and vanilla and mix to form a dough. Add the chocolate chips and mix well to incorporate.

2. Weigh the dough and divide into five equal portions. Roll each portion into a ball and transfer to an airtight container. Pop in the fridge for at least 24 hours and up to five days.

3. To make the peach filling, cut a shallow cross in the bottom of each peach. Place the peaches into simmering water for 1–2 minutes, remove and allow to cool slightly – the skin should start to lift away from the peaches. When cool enough to handle, peel the skins away and discard.

4. Chop the peach flesh into 2cm (¾in) chunks and place into a saucepan with the sugar and lemon juice. Heat over a low heat for 30–45 minutes until reduced. Remove roughly half of the syrup (this is great drizzled on yoghurt) and refrigerate the remainder.

5. Meanwhile, preheat the oven to 190°C/170°C fan/375°F/Gas 5.

6. Line a large baking sheet with baking parchment. Arrange the five dough balls on the baking sheet and bake for 24 minutes until golden on top.

Recipe continues on page 86

Baking to Share

7. Remove the cookies from the oven and allow to cool for 5 minutes. Using a sharp knife, cut a square into the deepest part of the cookie. Use a teaspoon the excavate the hole, leaving a thin layer of cookie at the bottom.

8. Time to assemble! Transfer the chilled peach filling to a piping bag fitted with your favourite nozzle, then pipe a blob of peach filling into each cavity. Finish with a dollop of clotted cream.

GEORGE LOVES A TIP!

— The best thing about this recipe is that any peaches will do! From juicy ripe beauties to those flat peaches that kinda look like blobfish, you'll still get a great flavour when they're simmered down into a weak jam-esque consistency.

— I usually divide my cookie dough into bigger quantities than five, but the smaller the cookies are, the higher the chances of them cracking open when stuffing. If you get confident with your first batch, you can divide the mixture into seven instead.

— The peach filling isn't as thick or sweet as a jam, so don't worry if yours looks a little watery – those peach juices will taste amazing as they soak into the cookies!

PISTACHIO COOKIE MILLIONAIRES

Prep + baking time:
1 hour, plus chilling
Serves: 12

Pistachio is having a moment and it's slowly started seeping into supermarket bakes and desserts, but don't be fooled – they never taste as nice as homemade! I like the pistachios in this recipe to be coarsely chopped so I get a crunch with each mouthful, but you can blitz them up to a fine crumb if you prefer.

For the base:
150g (5¼oz) butter
120g (4½oz) caster sugar
80g (3oz) light brown sugar
140g (5oz) plain flour
85g (3oz) pistachios, coarsely chopped, plus 50g (2oz) left whole
½ tsp baking powder
¼ tsp bicarbonate of soda
1 tsp salt flakes
2 egg yolks

For the caramel layer:
500g (1lb 2oz) Thiccc Caramel (see page 22)

For the topping:
300g (10½oz) white chocolate, broken into pieces
200g (7oz) pistachio cream
50g (2oz) pistachios, chopped

1. Preheat the oven to 190°C/170°C fan/375°F/Gas 5. Grease and line a 20cm (8in) square cake tin.

2. To make the base, cream the butter and sugars together until light and fluffy. Add the flour, chopped pistachios, baking powder, bicarbonate of soda, salt and egg yolks and beat to form a dough.

3. Press into the lined tin, scatter with the whole pistachios and bake for 18–20 minutes until golden on top. Leave to cool.

4. Meanwhile, make the Thiccc Caramel following the method on page 22. Spread the Thiccc Caramel over the cooled cookie base and set aside.

5. To make the topping, melt the white chocolate in a bowl over a bain-marie. Add the pistachio cream and stir to incorporate.

6. Pour the chocolate and pistachio mixture over the Thiccc Caramel and sprinkle with the chopped pistachios, then refrigerate for 4 hours before slicing and serving.

GEORGE LOVES A TIP!

— Don't be put off by the amount of salt in this recipe – it really makes the pistachio flavour shine and doesn't take away from the taste of the bake.

— You can get lots of different brands of pistachio cream now but bear in mind, the higher the pistachio content the better the quality and depth of flavour.

ULTIMATE CROWD PLEASERS

I could've plonked the term 'dinner party' in the chapter title here but I hate it with every fibre of my being, so settled on crowd-pleasers instead. Although the same concept applies – these are recipes that are great for sharing, and perhaps more demanding than the previous chapter and a little more elegant in places, too. The main requisite was that I could picture me serving these recipes at a family occasion and at least 75 per cent of attendees would want to tuck in.

You're gonna want to chastise me here… I've gone heavy on the cheesecakes in this chapter, and I'm pretty sure I've been vocal on my socials about having disdain for recipe books that give you ten different variations of the same recipe. BUT these ones are all unique enough to warrant their place! We've got a twist on millionaire's shortbread on page 96, cheesecake with a rocky road base on page 109, and cheesecake in a cake on page 115 (I might buy shares in Philadelphia or invest in a herd of cows), so don't come for me because I put in the work with these!

Milkybar Funfetti Cookie Sandwiches	93
Pistachio Rolls	94
Millionaire's Shortbread Cheesecake	96
Sticky Toffee Tart	99
Pistachio Tart	100
Pecan Pie + Salted Caramel Cake	103
Piña Colada Pie	105
Biscoff Rocky Road Cheesecake	109
Apple Pie + Custard Cake	110
Dairy Milk Millionaire Brownies	113
Blueberry + Lemon Cheesecake Cake	115

Ultimate Crowd Pleasers

MILKYBAR FUNFETTI COOKIE SANDWICHES

Prep + baking time:
45 mins, plus cooling
Serves: 5

These cookie sandwiches are one of the easiest recipes to bake yet are always one of the most popular! It's best to invest in higher quality sprinkles so the colours are still bright when baked and don't bleed into the mixture.

For the cookies:
150g (5¼oz) butter
120g (4½oz) light brown sugar
80g (3oz) caster sugar
2 egg yolks
225g (8oz) plain flour
½ tsp salt flakes
½ tsp baking powder
¼ tsp bicarbonate of soda
½ tsp vanilla bean paste
200g (7oz) Milkybar buttons
50g (2oz) funfetti sprinkles

For the buttercream:
100g (3½oz) Milkybar chocolate, broken into pieces
250g (9oz) butter
500g (1lb 2oz) icing sugar
25g (1oz) funfetti sprinkles

For the ganache:
300g (10½oz) Milkybar chocolate, broken into pieces
150g (5¼fl oz) double cream

To decorate:
50g (2oz) Milkybar chocolate, broken into pieces
Funfetti sprinkles

1. Preheat the oven to 190°C/170°C fan/375°F/Gas 5 and line two large baking sheets with baking parchment.

2. To make the cookies, cream the butter and sugars together until fluffy. Add the egg yolks, flour, salt, baking powder, bicarbonate of soda and vanilla and mix to form a dough. Add the Milkybar buttons and sprinkles and mix to incorporate.

3. Weigh the dough then divide it into ten equal portions, then roll each potion into a ball. Place five dough balls onto each baking tray, spacing the dough well apart, then bake for 10–12 minutes until the edges are golden. Transfer to a wire rack to cool.

4. To make the buttercream, melt the Milkybar in a bowl over a bain-marie, stirring until smooth. Beat the butter until pale and creamy then add the icing sugar and beat again until smooth. Pour the melted Milkybar into the bowl with the butter and icing sugar and beat until smooth and well combined. Add the sprinkles and mix to combine, then set aside.

5. To make the ganache, melt the Milkybar chocolate in a bowl over a bain-marie, stirring until smooth. Pour in the cream and beat until smooth and glossy.

6. Spoon the buttercream into a piping bag and snip off the end. Flip half of the cookies upside-down and pipe a dam of buttercream around the edges. Fill the craters with the ganache then top with the un-iced cookies.

7. To decorate, melt the Milkybar chocolate in a bowl over a bain-marie, stirring until smooth. Drizzle the cookie sandwiches with the melted chocolate and sprinkle with the funfetti.

GEORGE LOVES A TIP!

— The funfetti sprinkles in the buttercream make it tricky to use a nozzle when piping as they'll only get stuck in it, so just snip the end of the piping bag off and pipe straight through the hole instead of being too fancy.

— The cookies will set at room temperature and are best enjoyed that way, but refrigerating them in an airtight container will make them last much longer.

PISTACHIO ROLLS

Pistachio is a firm favourite of mine (mostly in dip form with feta, loads of herbs and chilli) because I like a sweet and salty dessert, and to be pretentious. These rolls are just that – cinnamon rolls but better. Don't be tempted to smother the tops in pistachio cream though, as it gets very sickly, very fast, and like these rolls, it's very moreish!

Prep + baking time: 3 hours
Serves: 12

For the dough:
500ml (17fl oz) whole milk
125g (4½oz) butter, plus extra for greasing
15g (½oz) fast-action dried yeast
125g (4½oz) caster sugar
750g (1lb 10oz) plain flour, plus extra for dusting
1 tsp baking powder
1 tsp salt flakes

For the pistachio filling:
300g (10½oz) pistachios
300g (10½oz) butter
200g (7oz) light brown sugar

For the pistachio frosting:
280g (9½oz) cream cheese, at room temperature
125g (4½oz) pistachio cream
250g (9oz) icing sugar
50ml (2fl oz) whole milk

To decorate:
75g (2¾oz) pistachios (optional)

1. To make the dough, warm the milk in a small saucepan over a medium heat until the temperature on a thermometer reaches 38–40°C (100–104°F). Meanwhile, melt the butter in a separate saucepan.

2. Tip the yeast and sugar into a large mixing bowl. Pour the warmed milk and melted butter over the yeast and sugar and stir to combine. Cover with cling film and leave the yeast to bloom somewhere warm for 10–15 minutes.

3. Once the yeasty milk mix has bloomed (it'll kinda look like a brain!), add 400g (14oz) of the flour and gently mix to form a wet dough. Cover again and place back in the warm place for an hour until doubled in size.

4. Meanwhile, line two 32 x 20cm (12½ x 8in) baking trays and then butter the lined sides (you could also use buttered foil trays).

5. Add the remaining flour, baking powder and salt to the wet dough, adding slightly more flour if required, and bring together to form a firmer dough. I like to use the handle of a wooden spoon for this, but you can also decant the dough onto a floured work surface and incorporate the ingredients with your hands.

6. Flour your work surface, hands and rolling pin. Tip the dough onto the work surface and roll out to a 35 x 70cm (14 x 27½in) rectangle.

7. To make the pistachio filling, blitz the pistachios to a paste in a food processor or blender – this will take at least 5 minutes and you may need to give your blender or food processor breaks so it doesn't overheat! You're looking for a fine paste that's slightly oily. Once achieved, add the butter and blitz again until combined.

8. Spread the pistachio filling over the dough rectangle then sprinkle over the brown sugar. Starting with the edge furthest away from you, roll the dough towards you to create a long roll, rolling as tightly as you can. If your roll has tapered ends, push and smush them in slightly to neaten.

9. Measure the roll and gently add shallow cuts to mark 12 even portions, then use dental floss to cut the dough into 12 rolls. Place six of the rolls, seam-side up, into each lined baking tray. Cover with cling film and leave to prove in a warm place for an hour.

10. Once your rolls have proved for 45 minutes, preheat the oven to 180°C/160°C fan/350°F/Gas 4.

11. Meanwhile, make the frosting. Beat the cream cheese and pistachio cream together until combined. Add the icing sugar and beat again until smooth. Slowly pour in the milk to loosen, mixing well after each addition, then set aside.

12. Bake the rolls for 23–28 minutes until lightly golden on top and puffy. Leave to cool for 5 minutes, then spread about three quarters of the frosting over the rolls, covering well. Drizzle with the remaining frosting just before serving.

GEORGE LOVES A TIP!

— Make sure your cream cheese is at room temperature when making your frosting to avoid any lumps.

— You'll have a little frosting left over after spreading it over the rolls, but it's great to drizzle over again when serving.

— Using dental floss to cut the rolls avoids damaging their shape.

— Instead of lining and buttering roasting tins, I like to use re-usable foil trays (that I place on baking trays when in the oven) to cook the rolls.

— You want your foil/baking trays to be at least 3cm (1¼in) deep (this is the standard size so don't worry too much!).

Ultimate Crowd Pleasers

MILLIONAIRE'S SHORTBREAD CHEESECAKE

I love millionaire's shortbread and could easily eat an entire tray without even realizing, so I decided to turn them into a proper dessert that would satisfy me with one serving. This cheesecake has a buttery shortbread base, a layer of rich caramel, creamy vanilla cheesecake and a thin layer of chocolate ganache that helps give this all the flavours of millionaire's shortbread but in a ginormous slice!

Prep + baking time:
1 hour plus chilling
Serves: 8

For the shortbread base:
130g (4¾oz) butter
175g (6oz) plain flour
50g (2oz) caster sugar

For the caramel:
400g (14oz) condensed milk
120g (4½oz) golden syrup
120g (4½oz) light brown sugar
175g (6oz) butter

For the cheesecake:
600g (1lb 5oz) cream cheese
300ml (10fl oz) double cream
125g (4½oz) icing sugar
1 tsp vanilla bean paste

For the ganache:
150g (5¼oz) milk chocolate, broken into pieces
75ml (2½fl oz) double cream

1. Preheat the oven to 160°C/140°C fan/320°F/Gas 3. Grease and line a 20cm (8in) round cake tin (see tip, below).

2. To make the shortbread base, rub the butter into the flour until the mixture resembles fine breadcrumbs. Add the sugar and use your hands to bring the mixture together to form a dough, then press the dough into the cake tin and bake for 20 minutes. Leave to cool.

3. Next, make your caramel layer! Heat the condensed milk, golden syrup, sugar and butter in a heavy-bottomed saucepan over a low heat, stirring until the sugar has dissolved. Turn the heat up to medium and whisk for 10–15 minutes until a thermometer reaches 103°C (217°C). Pour onto the cooled shortbread base and leave to set.

4. To make the cheesecake, whisk the cream cheese, cream, icing sugar and vanilla together for about 5 minutes until thiccc and creamy. Spoon onto the caramel layer and refrigerate for at least 4 hours until set.

5. To make the ganache, melt the chocolate in a bowl over a bain-marie, then add the cream and beat until smooth and glossy. Pour the ganache over the chilled cheesecake and smooth. Chill in the fridge for 15 minutes before serving.

GEORGE LOVES A TIP!

— Run a sharp knife under the hot tap before drying it and using it to slice the cheesecake, to ensure the ganache layer doesn't pull through the rest of the cheesecake.

— This cheesecake is very tall, so make sure the parchment paper is a few centimetres higher than the tin when lining it.

Ultimate Crowd Pleasers

STICKY TOFFEE TART

Prep + baking time:
2½ hours
Serves: 8

Ever fancied a sticky toffee pudding on the go without the mess? Of course you have. The sweet version of a Cornish pasty in my eyes, the pastry case is perfect to hold the pudding, enabling you to munch on the move, if ever you needed to. You're welcome.

For the pastry:
215g (7½oz) plain flour, plus extra for dusting
50g (2oz) light brown sugar
½ tsp salt
125g (4½oz) butter
1 egg

For the filling:
100g (3½oz) dates, roughly chopped
100ml (3½fl oz) whole milk
80g (3oz) butter
90g (3¼oz) light brown sugar
1 tbsp treacle
2 eggs
100g (3½oz) plain flour
½ tsp baking powder
½ tsp bicarbonate of soda
Pinch of salt
½ tsp vanilla

For the caramel:
325g (11½oz) condensed milk
85g (3oz) butter
60g (2¼oz) light brown sugar
30g (1⅛oz) golden syrup
30g (1⅛oz) treacle

1. Preheat the oven to 210°C/190°C fan/410°F/Gas 6.
2. To make the pastry, blitz together the flour, sugar and salt in a food processor until combined. Add the butter and egg and pulse until the dough comes together. Wrap the dough in cling film and chill for 20 minutes.
3. Turn the dough out onto a lightly floured work surface and roll out until 5mm (¼in) thick, then use the pastry to line a deep 22cm (9in) loose-bottomed tart tin and refrigerate for 20 minutes.
4. Line the chilled pastry case with parchment paper and fill with baking beans. Bake for 15 minutes, then remove the baking beans and parchment paper and bake for a further 5 minutes. Remove from the oven and reduce the oven temperature to 170°C/150°C fan/325°F/Gas 3.
5. To make the filling, place the dates into a small saucepan, pour over the milk and heat for 5 minutes over a low heat until the milk is steaming but not simmering. Remove from the heat and allow to cool slightly.
6. Cream the butter, sugar and treacle together until light and fluffy then add the eggs and mix to combine. Sieve in the flour and add the baking powder, bicarbonate of soda, salt and vanilla and beat to form a batter.
7. Pour the milk and date mixture into the batter and fold to combine, then pour the batter into the pastry case. Bake for 38 minutes then leave to cool.
8. To make the caramel, heat all the ingredients in a heavy-bottomed saucepan over a low heat, stirring occasionally, until melted. Increase the heat to medium-high and keep stirring as the caramel thickens and bubbles, until a thermometer reaches 103°C (217°C) (this can take up to 20 minutes).
9. Once achieved, pour the caramel onto the cooled tart and leave at room temperature to set before slicing and enjoying!

GEORGE LOVES A TIP!
— This tart is delicious cold because the caramel adds a layer of moisture to the tart, akin to sticky toffee sauce. That said, if you want to warm this up and douse it with even more Sticky Toffee Sauce (see page 26), it's gonna be even more delicious!

PISTACHIO TART

Prep + baking time:
3 hours plus chilling
Serves: 8

Pistachio pastry, pistachio cream, pistachio frangipane and pistachio whipped cream all combined into the ultimate pistachio tart that's perfect to make in advance for a crowd!

For the pistachio whipped cream:
400ml (13½fl oz) double cream
75g (3¾oz) pistachios

For the pastry:
50g (2oz) pistachios
200g (7oz) plain flour
30g (1⅛oz) icing sugar
110g (3¾oz) butter, diced
1 egg yolk

For the pistachio frangipane:
150g (5¼oz) pistachios
150g (5¼oz) butter
150g (5¼oz) caster sugar
3 eggs
225g (8oz) pistachio cream

1. To make the pistachio whipped cream, roughly chop the pistachios and roast for 10 minutes. Warm 225ml (7½fl oz) of the cream in a saucepan until steaming, then tip in the roasted pistachios and leave to infuse on the heat for 5 minutes. Transfer to a bowl and refrigerate.

2. To make the pastry, blitz the pistachios to a fine crumb in a food processor. Add the flour and icing sugar and blitz again to combine, then add the butter and egg yolk and pulse to form a dough. Wrap in cling film and refrigerate for 30 minutes.

3. Roll the dough out between two pieces of cling film until 5mm (¼in) thick then use the dough to line a 23cm (9in) loose-bottomed tart tin. Refrigerate for a further 20 minutes.

4. Meanwhile, preheat the oven to 210°C/190°C fan/410°F/Gas 6. Line the chilled pastry case with parchment paper and fill with baking beans. Bake for 15 minutes, then remove the baking beans and bake for a further 5 minutes. Remove from the oven and reduce the oven temperature to 180°C/160°C fan/350°F/Gas 4.

5. To make the pistachio frangipane, blitz the pistachios to a fine crumb in a food processor. Cream the butter and sugar together until light and fluffy then add the eggs and pistachios and mix to form a batter. Set aside.

6. Spoon the pistachio cream into the base of the pastry case and smooth out. Top with the frangipane and bake for 50 minutes until just a slight wobble remains. Leave to cool.

7. Remove the pistachio-infused cream from the fridge and strain through a sieve into a mixing bowl, using a spatula to push the cream through. Pour in the remaining 175ml (6fl oz) of double cream. Whisk until stiff, then dollop on top of your tart and spread to decorate.

GEORGE LOVES A TIP!
— To make this tart an even bigger showstopper, pipe the pistachio whipped cream on top and sprinkle with chopped pistachios.

PECAN PIE + SALTED CARAMEL CAKE

Prep + baking time: 2 hours
Serves: 12

I was really going through a phase of stuffing pies and tarts between cakes in 2016 and this cake was a natural successor to my Cherry Bakewell Cake – it even caught the eye of HRH King Charles, who met me at Ely Market! The pecan pie is slightly squishilicious, the pastry akin to a buttery shortbread and the buttercream sandwiching the cakes is sweet with a salty caramel kick, so this is perfect if you want a more balanced cake.

For the sponge:
300g (10½oz) butter
300g (10½oz) caster sugar
6 eggs
225g (8oz) self-raising flour
1½ tsp baking powder
75g (2¾oz) pecans, blitzed to a fine crumb

For the pecan pie:
250g (9oz) plain flour
125g (4½oz) butter, melted
250g (9oz) pecans, coarsely blitzed
4 eggs
100g (3½oz) light brown sugar
100g (3½oz) golden syrup
½ tsp vanilla bean paste

For the buttercream:
300g (10½oz) butter
600g (1lb 5oz) icing sugar
200g (7oz) Salted Caramel (see page 23)

1. Preheat the oven to 180°C/160°C fan/350°F/Gas 4 and grease and line two 20cm (8in) round cake tins.

2. To make the sponge, cream the butter and sugar together until light and fluffy. Add the eggs, flour, baking powder and pecans and mix to form a batter. Divide between the two tins and bake for 26–30 minutes until a skewer comes out clean. Leave to cool.

3. To make the pastry for the pecan pie, tip the flour into a bowl, add the melted butter and mix to form a dough. Push into a 20cm (8in) loose-bottomed tart tin with your hands, using your thumbs to push the pastry up the sides and into the fluted edges, then set aside.

4. To make the pecan pie filling, mix the pecans with the eggs, sugar, golden syrup and vanilla. Pour the mixture into the pastry case and bake for 28–32 minutes until golden on top. Set aside to cool completely.

5. Meanwhile, make the Salted Caramel following the method on page 23.

6. Once everything has cooled, it's time to assemble. To make the buttercream, beat the butter until pale and creamy. Add the icing sugar bit by bit, beating well after each addition until smooth. Add 50g (2oz) of the Salted Caramel and mix to combine.

7. Use the base of a cake tin as a guide to cut a 20cm (8in) round out of the middle of the pecan pie. Keep the edges for decoration.

Recipe continues on page 104

8. Spread the buttercream over the top of one of the sponges and place the pecan pie on top. Spread 75g (2¾oz) of the Salted Caramel over the pecan pie then top with the second sponge. Cover the sponge and pie stack with the remainder of the buttercream and set aside to allow the buttercream to set slightly.

9. Warm the remaining 75g (2¾oz) of Salted Caramel in a saucepan over a low heat, then drip over the cake. You can also use the caramel to help secure the cut-off edges of pecan pie around the rim of the cake, if you like.

GEORGE LOVES A TIP!

— Work the pastry into the tart tin while the mixture is still warm and malleable.
— When blitzing the pecans for the sponge, make sure not to overdo it or they'll turn into a nut butter and make the cake dense rather than light and fluffy.

PIÑA COLADA PIE

Prep + baking time:
4 hours plus chilling time
Serves: 12

Sipping a piña colada is the epitome of summer, which makes this the perfect, comforting summer dessert: pastry, coconut cream, pineapple cheesecake, doused with more pineapple curd and topped with Malibu meringue. Try not to eat the Malibu meringue by the spoonful – it's a dessert in itself!

For the pastry:
200g (7oz) plain flour, plus extra for dusting
30g (1⅛oz) ground almonds
40g (1½oz) icing sugar
125g (4½oz) cold butter, diced
1 large egg yolk
1 tbsp cold water

For the coconut cream filling:
50g (2oz) desiccated coconut
150ml (5¼fl oz) double cream
40g (1½oz) caster sugar
1 egg
30g (1⅛oz) plain flour
½ tsp vanilla bean paste

For the cheesecake:
450g (1lb) cream cheese
200g (7oz) double cream
75g (2¾oz) icing sugar
2 tbsp dark rum
1 quantity of Pineapple Curd (see tip on page 25)

1. To make the pastry, pulse the flour, ground almonds and icing sugar in a food processor until incorporated. Add the butter and egg yolk and pulse until combined, trickling the water in as you go to help form a dough, as needed. Tip the dough onto a lightly floured work surface and bring together with your hands, then roll the pastry out to a circle slightly larger than a 24.5cm (9¾in) deep, loose-bottomed tart tin. Use the pastry to line the tin then refrigerate for 30 minutes.

2. Preheat the oven to 210°C/190°C fan/410°F/Gas 6.

3. Cover the pastry base with a sheet of parchment paper and fill with baking beans. Blind bake for 15 minutes before removing the beans and parchment paper, then bake for a further 5 minutes. Remove the pastry case from the oven and set aside.

4. To make the filling, toast the coconut in a frying pan over a medium heat for 3–5 minutes until brown and fragrant, stirring often, then leave to cool.

5. Heat the cream, sugar, eggs, flour and vanilla in a heavy-bottomed saucepan over a medium heat, whisking for 10–15 minutes until thick and the consistency of white sauce. Add the toasted coconut, reserving a tablespoon for decorating, and stir to combine.

6. Pour the filling into the pastry case. Smooth to even out then return to the fridge while you make the Pineapple Curd and Rum Salted Caramel following the methods on pages 25 and 23.

7. To make the cheesecake, whisk the cream cheese, cream and icing sugar together in a large bowl until thick and creamy. Add the rum and 2 tablespoons of the Pineapple Curd and whisk until incorporated. Spoon the cheesecake over the coconut cream, smooth then refrigerate for at least 4 hours.

8. Reserve 2 tablespoons of the Pineapple Curd for decorating, then spoon the remainder over the cheesecake layer, smooth and set aside.

9. To make the Italian meringue, heat the water and sugar in a heavy-bottomed saucepan over a high heat to form a simmering syrup.

Recipe continues on page 107

Ultimate Crowd Pleasers

For the Italian meringue:
100ml (3½fl oz) water
150g (5¼oz) caster sugar
3 egg whites (approx. 120g/4½oz)
½ tsp cream of tartar
2 tbsp Malibu

To decorate:
1 quantity of Rum Salted Caramel (see tip on page 23)

10. Place the egg whites and cream of tartar into a mixing bowl and, when the syrup reaches 112°C (233°F), begin whisking the eggs on a low speed. When the syrup reaches 116°C (240°F), whisk on a medium speed. When the syrup reaches 120°C (250°F), turn the whisk up to high and slowly pour the syrup into the eggs, whisking until incorporated. Add the Malibu and continue whisking for 3–5 minutes until cool enough to handle.

11. Spoon the meringue into a piping bag and pipe the meringue over the top of the Pineapple Curd. Decorate with more Pineapple Curd, the remaining toasted coconut and my Rum Salted Caramel.

GEORGE LOVES A TIP!

— If you have a blowtorch, that's the perfect way to achieve the toasted meringue effect you see on page 106.

— The coconut toasts fast, so watch out!

BISCOFF ROCKY ROAD CHEESECAKE

Prep + baking time: 2 hours, plus chilling
Serves: 10

A regular Biscoff cheesecake is easy to make but hardly inspiring, so swapping the base (and adding sides) with a rocky road mixture makes this a much more exciting dessert!

For the rocky road:
375g (2¾oz) white chocolate, broken into pieces
75g (2¾oz) butter
200g (7oz) Biscoff spread
175g (6oz) Biscoff biscuits, crushed
75g (2¾oz) mini marshmallows

For the cheesecake filling:
500g (1lb 2oz) cream cheese
200g (7oz) Biscoff spread
100g (3½oz) icing sugar
300ml (10fl oz) double cream

1. Line a 24.5cm (9¾in) loose-bottomed, deep, fluted tart tin by cutting a slice of parchment paper slightly larger than the tin and scrunching it up. Unfurl the scrunched paper and push it into the tin's nooks and crannies.

2. To make the rocky road, melt the chocolate and butter together in a bowl over a bain-marie, stirring until smooth. Add the Biscoff spread and stir until melted and incorporated.

3. Toss the Biscoff biscuits and marshmallows together in a large bowl, pour over the chocolate mixture and toss well so everything is coated in chocolate.

4. Tip the rocky road mixture into the tin and top with another piece of parchment paper. Use your hands to smush the rocky road mixture around the sides of the tin to create as even a layer as possible. When you think you've achieved it, fill the lined tin with baking beans and refrigerate for at least 2 hours – the beans will help the rocky road to keep its shape.

5. To make the cheesecake filling, whisk the cream cheese, Biscoff spread, icing sugar and cream together for 3–5 minutes until thiccc and creamy.

6. Remove the rocky road from the fridge, take out the baking beans, peel away the parchment paper and fill the rocky road tart case with the cheesecake mixture. Return to the fridge for at least six hours before serving. Store in the fridge for up to five days.

GEORGE LOVES A TIP!

— Slicing this one can be a challenge. The cheesecake is best sliced straight from the fridge, but the rocky road is best sliced when brought back to room temperature. Therefore, it's best to heat a knife under hot running water for a minute or so before drying it and slicing. Repeating between cuts will keep the slices even and crumb-free.

APPLE PIE + CUSTARD CAKE

Prep + baking time:
2 hours, plus cooling and chilling
Serves: 14

It can be really hard to get apples into cakes without cooking them directly in the batter and masking with toffee or caramel flavours, but this never lets apples shine the way a pie or crumble does. So, this cake makes the most of getting a strong, sweet and tart flavour from the apples while creating a fresh, towering dessert that's perfect for sharing.

For the filling:
4 Bramley apples, approx. 500g (1lb 2oz)
2 tbsp water

For the sponge:
450g (1lb) butter
450g (1lb) caster sugar
9 eggs
450g (1lb) self-raising flour
2¼ tsp baking powder
20 drops custard flavouring

For the buttercream:
600g (1lb 5oz) butter
1.2kg (2lb 10oz) icing sugar
20 drops of custard flavouring
Green food colouring

1. Preheat the oven to 180°C/160°C fan/350°F/Gas 4. Line four 20cm (8in) round cake tins.

2. To make the filling, peel and core the apples then cut them into 1cm (½in) cubes. Place the apples and water in a medium saucepan over a low heat. Cover and cook for 30 minutes, stirring occasionally, until starting to break down and a knife can easily cut through any large chunks. Decant to a bowl and chill in the fridge.

3. To make the sponge, cream the butter and sugar together until light and fluffy. Add the eggs, flour and baking powder and beat to form a batter, then add the custard flavouring and stir through. Divide the batter between the four lined cake tins and bake for 18–22 minutes until a skewer comes out clean. Allow to cool.

4. To make the buttercream, beat the butter until pale and creamy. Add the icing sugar and beat again until smooth. Add the custard flavouring and mix to combine. Set aside 250g (9oz) of the buttercream.

5. Level the sponges using a serrated knife then spread a thin layer of buttercream onto the tops of three of the sponges.

6. Spoon a third of the buttercream into a piping bag, cut a 1cm (½in) hole in the end and pipe a thin dam of buttercream around the edges of the iced sponges. Don't worry if you haven't used all the buttercream.

7. Fill the craters with the stewed apples and stack the sponges on top of each other, topping with the un-iced sponge. Wrap the cake in cling film to stop it drying out then pop it in the fridge for at least 30 minutes for the buttercream to set.

8. Coat the cake with some of the remaining buttercream and smooth with a cake scraper or palette knife before returning to the fridge to firm up while you make your ombré buttercreams.

Recipe continues on page 112

Ultimate Crowd Pleasers

9. Place the reserved 250g (9oz) of buttercream back into the mixer and beat until white. Remove a fifth (roughly 50g/2oz) of the buttercream and set aside. Add a few drops of green food colouring, stir to combine then remove a quarter of the remaining buttercream and set aside. Add a few more drops of food colouring, stir to combine them remove a third of the remaining buttercream and set aside. Continue to create two further darker shades of green.

10. Remove the cake from the fridge and cover the bottom fifth with the darkest shade of green buttercream. Repeat with the remaining colours, moving up the cake with the lighter shades as you go, finishing with the white buttercream. Use any leftover white buttercream to cover the top of the cake.

11. Heat a cake scraper or palette knife in hot water, dry off and smooth around the cake to form a beautiful ombré effect.

GEORGE LOVES A TIP!

— You can add a spoonful of light brown sugar or cinnamon while stewing the apples for an extra dose of richness, but I love the sharp tartness paired with the fluffy custard buttercream.

DAIRY MILK MILLIONAIRE BROWNIES

Prep + baking time:
1½ hours, plus chilling
Serves: 16

These indulgent treats are the best way to upgrade your brownie and take it to the next level. A layer of Thiccc Caramel (see page 22) plus a smooth chocolate topping make these perfect for slicing into mini bites and enjoying at a party.

For the brownies:
200g (7oz) Dairy Milk chocolate, broken into pieces
250g (9oz) butter
300g (10½oz) caster sugar
4 eggs
80g (3oz) cocoa powder
65g (2½oz) plain flour
1 tsp salt flakes

For the topping:
200g (7oz) Dairy Milk chocolate, broken into pieces
400g (14oz) chocolate spread
500g (1lb 2oz) Thiccc Caramel (see page 22)

1. Preheat the oven to 180°C/160°C fan/350°F/Gas 4. Grease and line a 25cm (10in) square cake tin.

2. To make the brownies, melt the chocolate and butter together in a bowl over a bain-marie, stirring until smooth, then set aside to cool slightly.

3. Whisk the sugar and eggs together until thick, pale and almost doubled in size. Pour the melted chocolate and butter mixture into the eggs and continue to whisk until combined.

4. Add the cocoa powder, flour and salt, fold to combine then pour into the lined tin. Bake for 22–24 minutes until there's just a slight wobble on top, or when a thermometer reads 89°C (192°F). Leave at room temperature for 20 minutes before refrigerating for at least 90 minutes.

5. To make the topping, melt the chocolate and chocolate spread together in a small saucepan over a low heat.

6. Spread the Thiccc Caramel over the chilled brownie, then pour over the melted chocolate mixture. Refrigerate for at least four hours before slicing up and serving.

GEORGE LOVES A TIP!

— Add Mini Eggs into the brownie mixture and on top of the chocolate layer for an Easter vibe.

— Making the topping while the chocolate is still warm will create a glossier, smooth finish.

BLUEBERRY + LEMON CHEESECAKE CAKE

Prep + baking time:
1 hour plus setting time
Serves:
12–16

Baking blueberries into cakes is my favourite way to eat them, and adding sharp lemon curd layers between soothing cheesecake layers creates a taste sensation in your mouth!

For the sponge:
450g (1lb) butter
450g (1lb) caster sugar
Zest of 1 lemon
9 eggs
450g (1lb) self-raising flour
2⅓ tsp baking powder
250g (9oz) blueberries

For the buttercream:
600g (1lb 6oz) butter
1.2kg (2lb 7oz) icing sugar
Juice of half a lemon

For the cheesecake filling:
450g (1lb) cream cheese
200ml (6¾fl oz) double cream
75g (2¾oz) icing sugar
Juice of half a lemon
200g (7oz) Lemon Curd (see page 25)

To decorate:
250g (9oz) blueberries

1. Preheat the oven to 180°C/160°C fan/350°F/Gas 4 and line four 20cm (8in) round cake tins.

2. To make the sponge, cream the butter, sugar and lemon zest together for 3–5 minutes until light and fluffy. Add the eggs, flour and baking powder and beat until a batter forms. Fold the blueberries through the batter.

3. Divide the batter between the four lined tins and bake for 18–22 minutes until a skewer comes out clean. Allow to cool.

4. To make the buttercream, beat the butter until pale and creamy. Add the icing sugar and lemon juice and beat until smooth and soft.

5. To make the cheesecake filling, whisk the cream cheese, cream and icing sugar together for 3–5 minutes until thick. Add the lemon juice and fold through – it might seem a little sloppy but fear not, it will set when refrigerated.

6. Level the sponges using a serrated knife then spread buttercream over three of the sponges. Spoon a small amount of your buttercream into a piping bag, cut a 1cm (½in) hole in the end and pipe dams of buttercream around the edges of the three iced sponges. Repeat until the dams are about 2.5cm (1in) high.

7. Fill each of the craters with a third of the cheesecake mixture then smooth the surface so it's in line with the buttercream walls. Top each layer of cheesecake with the lemon curd and smooth over.

8. Stack the sponges on top of each another, finishing with the un-iced sponge. Wrap the cake in cling film and refrigerate for at least an hour to set.

9. Remove the cake from the fridge and cover the sides and top of the cake with the buttercream, using a cake scraper to smooth the edges. Arrange the blueberries on top of the cake and refrigerate until ready to serve.

GEORGE LOVES A TIP!

— While I like the blueberries in a layer at the bottom of each cake so that they're soaking up some of the lemon curd, if you want your blueberries evenly dispersed throughout the cake, toss them in a couple of tablespoons of flour before folding through the cake batter.

Ultimate Crowd Pleasers

SNUG SAVOURIES

Savoury baking, for me, is much more of a comfort than cooking sweet treats, and not just because my day-to-day is being surrounded by huge sacks of sugar, behaving like a cockalorum over cakes, swapping simmered sentences over cookie timings (it's never quite a heated discussion) and honking of brownies (people say it's amazing but it seeps into my clothes and doesn't align with my camomile-scented fantasy). It's more because it's so rare I have an occasion worthy of baking savouries for – the last thing I need is to be sitting in my cinema-cum-Lego room, chowing down on a platter piled with pastries.

When I do have such an occasion, it tends to be on the run up to Christmas when, if I get time off but am feeling too agitated to relax, I slip into a verklempt state where a salty mouthful is the only way to soothe the mind once more. That said, you can't beat a bit of pastry at a summer picnic or barbeque, and these recipes would be very welcome there, too.

Let it be known that my savoury recipes are constantly evolving (if I was ever to write a meal-based cookbook the damn thing would need an appendix to cover all the tangents I go off at and ways I would change, alter and adapt things). Without giving you all the different timings (because I'm lackadaisical and have to stop yabbering on somewhere), all of the individually portioned bakes in this chapter could totally be made larger to become part of a main meal.

And another thing… I also know that all of these savouries freeze amazingly! So even if you're baking these just for yourself, you can chuck them in the freezer and enjoy them again when you've had a long day at work/come home from a night out and your local fast-food joint* didn't hit the spot. (*Mine is best known for their spicy potatoes, which is ironic, because that's what I identify as if I stumble out of there after a pint of tequila and a kebab).

Shortcrust Pastry Case	120
Puff Pastry	121
Quiche Lorraine	123
Pear, Prosciutto, Gorgonzola + Walnut Quiche	124
Caprese Quiche	126
Roasted Grape + Goat's Cheese Scones	127
Pepperoni Pizza Focaccia	129
Harissa Sausage Rolls	131
Cranberry Brie + Bacon Rolls	132
Air Fryer Spring Rolls	135
Wild Garlic, Spinach, Ricotta + Lancashire Cheese Puffs	137
Pumpkin, Walnut, Sausage + Blue Cheese Pies	143
Roasted Fig, Prosciutto + Truffle Boursin Tart	144
Hot Honey, Jalapeno + Garlic Knots	147

SHORTCRUST PASTRY CASE

Prep + baking time:
45 minutes
Makes: 1 x 25cm (10in) round pastry case

This pastry case is the base for a few of my tart recipes and can easily be prepared in advance. The trick is to handle the pastry as little as possible while rolling out, and to fill the pastry case lining high with baking beans when blind baking.

225g (8oz) plain flour
½ tsp salt flakes
85g (3oz) cold butter, diced
1 egg yolk
1 tbsp cold water

1. Blitz the flour and salt together in a food processor to combine. Add the butter, egg yolk and water and pulse until the dough forms a ball. Wrap the dough in cling film and refrigerate for 20 minutes.

2. Roll the pastry out between two sheets of cling film to a circle slightly larger than a 25cm (10in) fluted tart tin. Remove the top layer of cling film and flip the pastry into the tart tin, pushing into the edges, nooks and crannies. Remove the remaining cling film and refrigerate for a further 20 minutes.

3. Preheat your oven to 210°C/190°C fan/410°F/Gas 6.

4. Line the pastry case with parchment paper and fill with baking beans. Bake for 25 minutes, then remove the baking beans and parchment paper and bake for a further 5 minutes.

PUFF PASTRY

Prep time:
45 minutes plus chilling time
Makes:
650g (1lb 7oz)

There are two major lies everyone has been telling you: the first is that money can't buy you happiness (it absolutely can, although it makes you even happier when others buy your happiness for you), and the second is that making your own pastry takes ages, is a faff and is no different to buying it from a shop. That's a load of Shiza Minnelli! Homemade puff pastry is crispier, pastryier, flakier, has better lamination than a display in a school corridor and really doesn't take too long to make. I make a big batch and freeze it for whenever I need an emergency sausage roll (which is often).

250g (9oz) butter, at room temperature
275g (10oz) plain flour
1 tsp salt flakes
135g (4¾oz) cold water

1. Remove the butter from the fridge 30 minutes before you want to make the pastry.

2. Blitz the flour and salt together in a food processor to combine, then, with the blade still running, slowly pour in the cold water until the dough starts to form a ball. Wrap in cling film and refrigerate for 30 minutes.

3. Remove from the fridge and roll into a rectangle, roughly 30 x 15cm (12 x 6in). Place the butter between two pieces of parchment paper and use a rolling pin to bash it, then roll out to a 15 x 10cm (6 x 4in) rectangle and place in the centre of the dough.

4. Fold the top third of the dough down and the bottom third up to cover it and create a new block. Refrigerate for 10 minutes.

5. Re-roll the pastry to a 30 x 15cm (12 x 6in) rectangle, being careful not to push the butter out of the sides, then fold the top third down and the bottom third up again. Repeat at least twice more before wrapping in cling film and refrigerating for at least 2 hours, then you're ready to use it!

GEORGE LOVES A TIP!
— I always keep a double batch of this in my freezer. To freeze, wrap the pastry tightly in cling film and make sure to thaw it out in the fridge to maintain the layers.

Snug Savouries

QUICHE LORRAINE

I recently saw what no doubt was a modern philosopher online, pondering why people will comfortably eat an entire pizza to little ridicule, yet, if you eat a whole quiche, you'll be judged and break social norms! It'd be hard not to eat this entire Quiche Lorraine as it's the most delicious you'll ever consume, but best to cook it for a crowd to avoid the embarrassment.

Prep + baking time:
1½ hours
Serves: 8

For the pastry:
1 Shortcrust Pastry Case (see page 120)

For the filling:
180g (5½oz) smoked bacon lardons
2 shallots, finely sliced
250g (9oz) cheddar cheese, grated
4 eggs
400ml (13½fl oz) double cream
Salt
Freshly ground black pepper

1. Make and bake the Shortcrust Pastry Case following the method on page 120 then reduce the oven temperature to 180°C/160°C fan/350°F/Gas 4.

2. To make the filling, tip the bacon lardons into a cold frying pan then place over a medium heat. Cook for 10–15 minutes until browned and the fat has rendered, then remove from the pan and set aside.

3. Add the shallots to the pan and cook in the bacon fat for 15 minutes until caramelized, then remove from the heat.

4. Tip the shallots into the pastry case followed by a third of the cheddar and half of the bacon lardons. Sprinkle over another third of the cheddar and the remaining lardons.

5. Break the eggs into a bowl, pour over the cream, season with salt and pepper then whisk to combine. Gently pour into the pastry case.

6. Top with the remaining cheddar and bake for 30–35 minutes until golden on top with a slight wobble in the middle. Leave to cool before serving.

Snug Savouries

PEAR, PROSCIUTTO, GORGONZOLA + WALNUT QUICHE

When I first approached my local council to trade at the farmers' markets, selling cakes by the slice, I was told that a stall full of sweet bakes wouldn't be accepted because there was already a baker at the market. So, to get onto the market, I proposed selling slices of quiche too, which they agreed to. This meant I had to come up with a few interesting flavours and this became my bestseller and personal favourite! The walnut pastry is easy to make and full of flavour, and the sweet-and-salty pairing of the pears and cheese in the filling is to die for. This is delicious hot, although my favourite way to eat it is cold the following day, once the cheese has set.

Prep + baking time: 1½ hours
Serves: 8

For the walnut pastry:
50g (2oz) walnuts
175g (6oz) plain flour
½ tsp salt flakes
85g (3oz) cold butter, diced
1 egg yolk
1 tbsp cold water

For the filling:
Knob of butter
1 shallot, finely sliced
3 conference pears
1 tbsp light brown sugar
2 springs of thyme, leaves only
175g (6oz) gorgonzola, torn into chunks
4 eggs
400ml (13½fl oz) double cream
9 slices (approx. 160g/5½oz) prosciutto
Salt and freshly ground black pepper

1. To make the walnut pastry, tip the walnuts, flour and salt into a food processor and blitz until the walnuts break down and are incorporated into the flour. Add the butter, egg yolk and cold water and pulse to form a dough. Roll the dough out between two sheets of cling film to a circle slightly larger than a 25cm (10in) fluted tart tin. Use the pastry to line the tin and refrigerate for 20 minutes.

2. Meanwhile, preheat the oven to 210°C/190°C fan/410°F/Gas 6.

3. Line the pastry case with parchment paper and fill with baking beans. Bake for 25 minutes then remove the baking beans and parchment paper and bake for a further 5 minutes.

4. To make the filling, heat the butter in a frying pan over a medium heat and fry the shallot for 15 minutes until caramelized. Peel and cube one of the pears and add to the pan. Cook for 5 minutes until softened, then add the sugar and half of the thyme leaves. Season and continue cooking for 3–5 minutes until the sugar has begun to caramelize. Spoon the shallot and pear mixture into the pastry case and dot half of the gorgonzola over the top.

5. Break the eggs into a bowl, pour over the cream, season with salt and pepper and whisk to combine. Gently pour into the pastry case.

6. Now for the fun decoration! Peel and quarter each of the remaining pears lengthways and remove the cores, then slice each quarter into three slices. Create a pattern on the top of the quiche by placing one slice of prosciutto followed by three slices of pear, carefully overlapping as you go. Repeat seven times until the pattern meets again, tucking the final pear slice under the first piece of prosciutto.

7. Shape the final slice of prosciutto into a 'flower' and place in the centre of the quiche. Dot the remaining gorgonzola around the edges of the quiche, with one chunk in the centre of the prosciutto flower. Sprinkle with the remaining thyme leaves and bake in the centre of the oven for 40–45 minutes until golden on top with a slight wobble in the middle.

8. Allow to cool for at least an hour before removing from the tart case, slicing and serving.

Pictured on page 122

CAPRESE QUICHE

Prep + baking time: 1½ hours
Serves: 8

First of all, who is paying for caprese salad in a restaurant? £8 for someone to chop up some tomato for you? Give over! Anyway, it's a classic flavour combination and we've crammed it in because it's veggie friendly which the other two quiche flavours aren't. I'm a snob so love to drizzle some balsamic over, to make it seem a bit posher.

For the pastry:
1 Shortcrust Pastry Case (see page 120)

For the filling:
450g (1lb) vine tomatoes, sliced
Salt flakes, for sprinkling
1 small bunch of basil (approx. 30g/1⅛oz)
250g (9oz) mozzarella, torn into chunks
4 eggs
400ml (13½fl oz) double cream
Salt and freshly ground black pepper
Balsamic vinegar, to serve (optional)

1. Make and bake the Shortcrust Pastry Case following the method on page 120, then reduce the oven temperature to 180°C/160°C fan/350°F/Gas 4.
2. Place the sliced tomatoes on a baking tray, sprinkle with salt flakes and roast for 20 minutes until slightly dehydrated.
3. Layer the roasted tomatoes, basil leaves and mozzarella into the pastry case.
4. Break the eggs into a bowl, pour over the cream, season with salt and pepper then whisk to combine. Gently pour into the pastry case.
5. Bake for 30–35 minutes until golden on top with a slight wobble in the centre. Allow to cool then serve with a drizzle of balsamic vinegar, if liked.

Pictured on page 122

ROASTED GRAPE + GOAT'S CHEESE SCONES

Coming out of the first Covid-19 lockdown, I had just moved into my first big baking unit and spent most of my time organizing and kitting it out with my mum, Lady Jayne, and sister, Sami. We would have a well-earned rest each day over a delicious lunch from one of my many cookbooks. One of our favourites was a goats' cheese and roast grape tartine from Diana Henry's Simple, so I wanted to take the flavours from that recipe and turn them into something Sami could make at home. And here it is!

Prep + baking time:
1 hour
Serves: 16–18

For the grapes:
500g (1lb 2oz) seedless black grapes
½ tsp salt flakes
2 tbsp balsamic vinegar
1 tbsp extra virgin olive oil

For the scones:
300g (10½oz) buttermilk, plus extra for glazing
650g (1lb 7oz) self-raising flour, plus extra for dusting
1 tsp salt flakes
Black pepper, to taste
300g (10½oz) goat's cheese, chopped
125g (4½oz) butter, diced

1. Preheat the oven to 200°C/180°C fan/400°F/Gas 6 and line two large baking trays.

2. Toss the grapes with the salt, vinegar and olive oil and place onto one of the baking trays. Roast for 25–30 minutes, tossing halfway through, until shrivelled, fragrant and juicy. Set aside to cool.

3. To make the scones, warm the buttermilk in a small saucepan over a low heat until just warmed.

4. Combine the flour, salt and pepper in a mixing bowl. Add the butter and rub in until the mixture resembles coarse breadcrumbs. Add the goat's cheese and combine.

5. Tip the roasted grapes and their juices into the mixing bowl and toss through to coat with flour. Pour in the buttermilk and mix to combine, pushing the mixture together to form a dough.

6. Turn the dough out onto a floured work surface and pat together until about 7¾cm (3in) thick. Use a 7¾cm (3in) round pastry cutter to cut out 16–18 scones, pushing the dough back together after each round of cuts as needed.

7. Use your thumb to coat the top of each scone with a glaze of buttermilk then bake for 20–25 minutes until golden, with the cheese and the grapes bleeding through the dough.

GEORGE LOVES A TIP!

— Both hard and soft goat's cheese will work in this recipe, just make sure to toss it well in the flour so it doesn't get smushed into the dough with the buttermilk.

— Heating the buttermilk makes it easier to form the dough and adhere everything together.

Snug Savouries

PEPPERONI PIZZA FOCACCIA

Prep + baking time:
1 hour, plus proving time
Serves: 6

This is essentially a deep dish pizza, infused with the pizza toppings as well as being smothered in them!

For the focaccia:
500g (1lb 2oz) strong bread flour
1 tsp salt flakes
1 tsp garlic salt
7g (¼oz) dried yeast
45g (1½oz) pizza sauce
450ml (15fl oz) warm water
1 tsp dried oregano
125g (4½oz) mozzarella cheese
100g (3½oz) pepperoni

For the topping:
155g (5½oz) pizza sauce
½ bunch fresh basil
150g (5½oz) mozzarella
100g (3½oz) pepperoni

1. Make the dough by placing the flour in a large mixing bowl. Add the yeast and salts to opposite sides of the bowl. Mix the pizza sauce and warm water together before pouring into the dough and kneading for 5 minutes until it forms a sloppy dough. Add in the oregano, 125g (4½oz) cheese and 100g (3½oz) pepperoni and knead through the dough. Place into a bowl and drizzle oil around the edges to allow the dough to rise as it proves. Place in the fridge overnight.

2. Lightly oil a 30x15cm baking tin. Remove the dough from its bowl in the fridge and place in the oiled tin, gently pulling it to fill the tin size as much as possible, then cover with cling film and leave to rise, somewhere warm, for 3-4 hours.

3. Preheat the oven to 180°C/160°C fan/350°F/Gas 4.

4. Uncover the risen dough and cook for 25-30 minutes until starting to turn golden on top. Remove from the oven and quickly spoon and spread over the pizza sauce, topping with torn basil leaves, cheese and finally the pepperoni.

5. Turn the oven up to 200°C/180°C fan/400°F/Gas 6 and cook for a further 5-10 minutes until melted and golden to your satisfaction!

GEORGE LOVES A TIP!

— The water for your dough should be between 38-40°C (100-104°F).

— This makes an amazing bread for a sandwich!

— The simplest way to make your own pizza sauce is to heat 250ml (9oz) passata, 1 tsp garlic salt, 2 tsp dried oregano and a good crank of black pepper together until slightly reduced and thick.

HARISSA SAUSAGE ROLLS

I'm sure everyone has their own way of making sausage rolls, but these are a fairly basic yet tasty variation you may not have tried before. If you can't get hold of sausage meat, just skin some sausages. Do try this with my Puff Pastry recipe (see page 121), as I promise you really can tell the difference. These can be frozen before or after cooking and are so handy to have in the freezer on standby.

Prep + baking time:
45 minutes
Serves: 12

For the pastry:
1 quantity of Puff Pastry (see page 121)
Flour, for dusting

For the filling:
1 tsp olive oil
1 shallot, finely diced
350g (12¼oz) sausage meat
1 tbsp harissa paste (I like rose or apricot harissa)
½ tsp dried oregano
1 egg, beaten, plus 1 yolk
1 tsp salt flakes

1. Make the Puff Pastry following the method on page 121 then preheat the oven to 180°C/160°C fan/350°F/Gas 4.

2. To make the filling, heat the olive oil in a medium frying pan over a medium heat, add the shallots and fry for about 10 minutes until caramelized. Leave to cool.

3. Place the sausage meat, harissa paste, oregano, egg yolk, salt and cooled shallots into a mixing bowl and mix until combined (using your hands, if easier) then set aside.

4. Tip the pastry onto a lightly floured work surface and roll out to a 30 x 20cm (12 x 8in) rectangle, and then cut in half lengthways to form two 30 x 10cm (12 x 4in) rectangles.

5. Leave a 1cm (½in) gap before placing a line of the sausage filling across the pastry. Use some of your beaten egg to wet the 1cm (½in) gap next to the sausage filling, before folding over the pastry. Use a fork to seal the two pastry edges together, or crimp together, before slicing into 5cm (2in) sections. Place the rolls on a baking tray and glaze with more beaten egg.

6. Bake for 20–22 minutes until flaky and golden on top.

GEORGE LOVES A TIP!

— Nothing beats eating these warm, but they'll also store in the fridge, in an airtight container, for up to three days.

— You could sprinkle the sausage rolls with poppy, sesame or even nigella seeds before baking.

Snug Savouries

CRANBERRY, BRIE + BACON ROLLS

Cranberry, brie and bacon is one of the most comforting winter combinations, and not just for toasties – it works amazingly as savoury rolls, too! Not as sweet as you'd expect and with melty cheese that sinks through the dough as it cooks, these are extremely indulgent. The bacon butter is inspired (not that I'm biased) and you can enjoy it in a number of different ways, especially in a sausage sandwich spread on the slice of bread you haven't smothered in HP sauce.

Prep + baking time:
3 hours
Serves: 12

For the dough:
500ml (17fl oz) whole milk
125g (4½oz) butter, plus extra for greasing
15g (½oz) fast-action dried yeast
750g (1lb 10oz) plain flour, plus extra for dusting
1 tsp salt
1 tsp baking powder

For the filling:
200g (7oz) cranberry sauce
150g (5¼oz) butter, softened
300g (10½oz) brie, finely sliced or grated

For the topping:
240g (8¼oz) bacon
150g (5¼oz) butter

1. To make the dough, warm the milk in a small saucepan over a medium heat until the temperature on a thermometer reaches 38–40°C (100–104°C). Meanwhile, melt the butter in a separate saucepan.

2. Sprinkle the yeast into a large mixing bowl then pour the warmed milk and melted butter over the yeast and stir to combine. Cover with cling film and leave the yeast to bloom somewhere warm for 10–15 minutes.

3. Once the yeasty milk mix has bloomed (it'll kinda look like a brain!), add 400g (14oz) of the flour and gently mix to form a very wet dough. Cover again and place back in the warm place for an hour until doubled in size.

4. Meanwhile, line two 32 x 20cm (12½ x 8in) baking trays with baking parchment then butter the lined sides (you could also use buttered foil trays).

5. Add the remaining flour, baking powder and salt to the wet dough. Mix to form a firmer dough, adding slightly more flour if required. (You might find it easier to decant the dough onto a floured work surface and incorporate the ingredients with your hands.)

6. Flour your work surface, hands and rolling pin. Tip the dough onto the work surface and roll out to a 35 x 70cm (14 x 27½in) rectangle.

7. To make the filling, mix the cranberry sauce with the butter. Spread the cranberry mixture over the dough then scatter over the brie.

8. Starting with the edge furthest away from you, roll the dough towards you to create a long roll, rolling as tightly as possible. If your roll has tapered ends, just push them and smush them up slightly so the roll is roughly even in width.

9. Measure the roll and gently make shallow cuts to divide it into 12 portions, then use dental floss to cut the dough into 12 rolls. Place six of the rolls, seam-side up, into each lined baking tray. Cover with cling film and leave to prove in a warm place for an hour.

Recipe continues on page 134

Snug Savouries

10. Once your rolls have proved for 45 minutes, preheat the oven to 180°C/160°C fan/350°F/Gas 4.

11. Fry the bacon in a large frying pan over a medium heat and cook for 15–20 minutes until crispy. Drain on kitchen paper and pat dry, then tip into a food processor and blitz to a fine crumb. Add the butter and blitz until combined, then set aside.

12. Remove the cling film from the rolls and bake for 23–28 minutes until puffy, golden and oozing with cranberry and cheese. While still warm, spread the bacon butter over the rolls and allow it to melt onto and into the rolls.

GEORGE LOVES A TIP!

— If you're looking for a warm spot to leave your dough to rise, try popping it on top of a high shelf or in a warm airing cupboard – or if all else fails, your kitchen work surface should do the trick, too.

— I like to use the handle of a wooden spoon to bring my dough together without getting myself into a sticky mess!

AIR FRYER SPRING ROLLS

I recently went to Disney World and stomped my way around the park trying to find a spring roll stand I'd seen on social media. After buying myself some pepperoni pizza and cheeseburger spring rolls, I was in love. They're one of the greatest creations ever and so easy to make. I used to be totally against air fryers but air frying is the fastest and best way to cook them. I've had to climb down from my judgemental high horse and order an air fryer purely to cook them. Hundreds have since been made and eaten – here's my two favourites.

Prep + baking time:
15 minutes
Serves: 15

300g (10½oz) ham, chopped
200g (7oz) cheddar cheese, cut into 7 x 2cm (2¾ x ¾in) slices
50g (2oz) pickled onions, cut into eighths
100g (3½oz) sweet pickle
15 spring roll wrappers

PLOUGHMAN'S SPRING ROLLS

1. Sprinkle ham, a slice of cheese, 3 slices of pickled onions and a teaspoon of pickle on the centre of a wrapper, leaving the outer 2.5cm (1in) uncovered.

2. Fold the wrapper down and up over the filling, then fold each side in so that the roll is as wide as the filling. Begin to roll the cigar-shaped wrapper up until you're about 2.5cm (1in) from the end.

3. Dab the exposed wrapper with cold water and fold to seal. Repeat with the remaining ingredients.

4. Air fryer cook for 10 minutes at 200°C (400°F) until oozing and delicious.

Prep + baking time:
15 minutes
Serves: 15

200g (7oz) pepperoni
1 bunch of basil
200g (7oz) mozzarella cheese, sliced
15 spring roll wrappers
100g (3½oz) pizza sauce (see tip on page 129), or use ready-made

PEPPERONI PIZZA SPRING ROLLS

1. Place a few slices of pepperoni, a couple of basil leaves and a slice of cheese onto one of the wrappers. Smear a tablespoon of sauce next to the cheese.

2. Fold the excess wrapper from the left- and right-hand sides in to the middle of the roll, to form a long rectangle. Roll the wrapper and filling all the way up, stopping about 2.5cm (1in) from the end.

3. Dab the final bit of exposed wrapper with cold water, then roll once more to seal together. Repeat with the remaining ingredients.

4. Air fry for 10 minutes at 200°C (400°F) until crisp and bubbling.

GEORGE LOVES A TIP!

— I was about 130% shook when I discovered spring rolls weren't made in filo pastry. Turns out there's specific spring roll pastry and you can buy sheets of it, in packs of 30, from supermarkets in the freezer aisle. I'll never not have it in my freezer again.

WILD GARLIC, SPINACH, RICOTTA + LANCASHIRE CHEESE PUFFS

Prep + baking time:
40 minutes
Serves: 14

Wild garlic is a herb foraged in British springtime that has a beautiful and distinct flavour. It's been trending so much of late that you can now buy it in packets from the freezer aisle from the posher supermarkets. Quite a small amount goes a long way.

For the pastry:
1 quantity of Puff Pastry (see page 121)
Flour, for dusting

For the filling:
125g (4½oz) spinach
125g (4½oz) ricotta cheese
150g (5¼oz) Lancashire cheese, grated
1 tbsp chopped wild garlic
1 tsp salt flakes
1 egg, beaten, plus 2 yolks
75g (2¾oz) Parmesan cheese, grated

1. Make the Puff Pastry following the method on page 121 then preheat the oven to 180°C/160°C fan/350°F/Gas 4 and line two large baking trays.

2. To make the filling, heat the spinach in a large pan over a medium heat until just wilted, then allow to cool slightly and squeeze out any excess moisture using your hands.

3. Place the spinach into a mixing bowl with the ricotta, Lancashire cheese, wild garlic, salt flakes and egg yolks and mix until combined using a fork. Set aside.

4. Tip the pastry onto a lightly floured work surface and roll out to a 32 x 32cm (12½ x 12½in) square. Cut the large pastry square into 16 smaller squares measuring 8 x 8cm (3¼ x 3¼in).

5. Fold each pastry shape in half to form an isosceles triangle, then cut two lines 5cm deep towards the apex of the triangle, along the legs of the triangle, about 1cm from the edge – see the photos overleaf. Unfurl the pastry back into a square and turn to form a diamond shape.

6. Spoon a dollop of the spinach and cheese mixture into the middle of each pastry square then fold the strips, one at a time, to form a pretty pastry shape, known as a duchess. Brush the pastry with the beaten egg then sprinkle with the Parmesan.

7. Place the rolls onto the lined baking trays and bake for 30 minutes until puffed, golden and oozing with cheese… enjoy!

GEORGE LOVES A TIP!

— If you're on a time crunch, sub out making the puff pastry for a shop-bought one.

Snug Savouries

CHEESE BISCUITS

Prep + baking time:
30 minutes
Serves: 16–20

No, they're not scones! But these cheese biscuits do slightly resemble them. In truth, they're flakier than a scone but the layers melt together like pastry. Whatever they are, they're absurdly addictive. I like them warm on their own but smearing chutney over them and topping with a slice of cheese will also have you shovelling them in.

350g (12¼oz) plain flour, plus extra for dusting
50g (2oz) wholemeal flour
1 tsp nigella seeds
50g (2oz) spring onions, finely sliced
1 tsp salt flakes
200g (7oz) butter
175g (6oz) cheddar cheese, grated
125g (4½oz) feta cheese
200g (7oz) soured cream
Milk, for brushing

1. Preheat the oven to 190°C/170°C fan/375°F/Gas 5 and line a large baking sheet with baking parchment.

2. Place both flours, nigella seeds, spring onions and salt into a bowl and toss to combine. Add the butter and rub in until no lumps of butter remain.

3. Add the grated cheddar and crumble in the feta then toss to coat with the flour mixture. Add the soured cream and mix to form a dough, pushing the mixture together so as not to work the dough too much.

4. Lightly flour your work surface and roll the dough out to a thickness of 2.5cm (1in), then use a 5cm (2in) round cutter to cut circles from the dough. Place the dough circles onto the lined baking sheet.

5. Brush the top of the biscuits with milk and bake for 20 minutes until golden brown and flaky.

GEORGE LOVES A TIP!

— I like to use a fluted cutter to give maximum surface area for browned edges, which are my favourite part of these cheesy biscuits.

Snug Savouries

PUMPKIN, WALNUT, SAUSAGE + BLUE CHEESE PIES

I'm OBSESSED with this flavour combo and usually make it as a pasta sauce after a cold winter market, but these pies are even more luxurious and a great way to package up the gorgeous filling. Any squash will work just fine – crown prince and kabocha are my personal favourites, but I'll settle for whatever I can get my hands on. I also love using a creamier blue cheese (Saint Agur, Cambozola or Fourme d'Ambert are my picks), but since you're melting with cream cheese, any will work just fine.

Prep + baking time:
1 hour
Serves: 6

For the pastry:
1 quantity of Puff Pastry (see page 121)
Flour, for dusting

For the filling:
500g (1lb 2oz) pumpkin or squash of your choice, peeled and cut into 2cm (¾in) cubes
2 tbsp olive oil
½ tsp salt flakes
400g (14oz) sausages
160g (5½oz) cream cheese
150g (5¼oz) blue cheese
100g (3½oz) walnuts, chopped
1 egg, beaten

1. Make the Puff Pastry following the method on page 121. Preheat the oven to 180°C/160°C fan/350°F/Gas 4. Grease and line a large baking tray.

2. Place the pumpkin into a roasting tin and drizzle with 1 tablespoon of the oil. Sprinkle over the salt and cook for 30 minutes until softened.

3. Meanwhile, heat the remaining 1 tablespoon of oil in a frying pan over a medium-high heat. Peel the skins from the sausages and tear clumps into the frying pan. Fry until golden brown.

4. Add the cream cheese and warm through then crumble or tear in the blue cheese and stir to combine. Add the pumpkin to the mixture once cooked.

5. Toast the walnuts in a separate dry frying pan over a high heat for 3–5 minutes until fragrant. Tip into a mixing bowl and add the cheesy pumpkin and sausage mixture. Stir to combine.

6. Lightly flour your work surface and roll the pastry out until 5mm (¼in) thick. Use a 8cm (3¼in) pastry cutter to cut out six rounds. Place the pastry rounds onto the lined baking tray and top each with a spoonful of the cheesy pumpkin and sausage mixture.

7. Roll the pastry out again and cut out six 10cm (4in) wide circles. Place the larger pastry circles over the smaller ones and use a fork to press the edges together.

8. Brush each pie with the beaten egg and bake for 22 minutes until golden and puffed.

ROASTED FIG, PROSCIUTTO + TRUFFLE BOURSIN TART

Prep + baking time:
45 minutes
Serves: 6

This is a quick and simple way to whip up a delicious tart for a special occasion, or even just for tea.

For the pastry:
1 quantity of Puff Pastry (see page 121)
Flour, for dusting

For the filling:
150g (5¼oz) truffle Boursin cheese
80g (3oz) prosciutto (approx. 6 slices), torn into pieces
3 figs
1 egg, beaten

To serve:
Balsamic vinegar

1. Make the Puff Pastry following the method on page 121.
2. Preheat the oven to 190°C/170°C fan/375°F/Gas 5. Grease and line a large baking sheet.
3. Turn the pastry out onto a floured work surface and roll out to a 30 x 20cm (12 x 8in) rectangle, then transfer to the baking sheet. Fold 1cm (½in) of the pastry over around the edges to create a border.
4. To fill the tart, spread the Boursin over the pastry, avoiding the border. Lay the prosciutto over the cheese. Slice the figs in quarters then half each quarter again so you have eight thin slices from each fig. Arrange on top of the prosciutto.
5. Brush the pastry border with the beaten egg then bake for 20–24 minutes until puffed up and golden. Serve drizzled with balsamic vinegar.

GEORGE LOVES A TIP!
— Discard the jalapeño seeds if you don't want too much heat!

HOT HONEY, JALAPEÑO + CHEESY GARLIC KNOTS

I don't know about you, but whenever I see a recipe calling for one or two cloves of garlic, I know it really means at least six, so I've pushed the boat out and used an entire bulb here to save you precious peeling time. These knots will really elevate your average garlic bread side (although they're a snack in their own right, if you ask me… I ate nine the first time I made them) – just don't be planning on kissing anyone after eating a few of these!

Prep + baking time: 3 hours
Serves: 15

For the dough:
7g (¼oz) fast-action dried yeast
1 tsp sugar
50g (2oz) butter, melted
300ml (10fl oz) warm water
1 tsp salt
525g (1lb 2½oz) plain flour, plus extra for dusting

For the filling:
1 garlic bulb
1 tsp extra virgin olive oil
1 tsp salt
200g (7oz) salted butter
1 tbsp chopped parsley
3 jalapeño chillies, finely chopped
250g (9oz) Cheddar cheese, grated
50g (2oz) honey

1. Preheat the oven to 180°C/160°C fan/350°F/Gas 4.
2. To make the dough, mix the yeast, sugar and melted butter into a jug with the water. Cover with cling film and leave somewhere warm for 10 minutes to activate the yeast.
3. Combine the salt and flour in a large bowl. Pour the yeast mixture over the flour and mix to form a dough. Transfer to a clean bowl, cover with cling film and leave in a warm place to rise for about an hour.
4. Meanwhile, make the filling. Cut the garlic bulb in half and place on a piece of tin foil, cut side up. Drizzle with the oil, sprinkle over the salt, scrunch the foil to cover the garlic and roast for 45 minutes until golden, then leave to cool slightly.
5. Squeeze the garlic cloves out of their skins then mash with the butter and parsley.
6. Once the dough has risen, knead for a couple of minutes then turn out onto a lightly floured work surface and roll out to a 50 x 30cm (20 x 12in) rectangle.
7. If necessary, turn the dough so a shorter edge is closest to you, then spread three quarters of the garlic butter over the bottom half of the dough. Sprinkle over the jalapeño chillies and cheese then fold the uncovered dough over the covered half, pressing to stick everything together.
8. Use a knife or pizza cutter to cut the dough into 15 long strips. Tie the strips into knots, tucking the edges of the dough underneath so they don't unfurl while cooking. Bake for 20–22 minutes until golden.
9. Meanwhile, melt the remaining garlic butter with the honey in a small saucepan over a low heat, stirring to combine.
10. As soon as the knots come out of the oven, brush with the hot honeyed garlic butter and serve.

Snug Savouries

There's so much bombastic rhetoric around indulgent desserts and puddings, mainly from supermarkets overselling their autumnal wares, that I feel the true meaning of a good pudding has been lost. In my eyes this is also partly due to the desire to turn everything into a little sweet treat (a tiramisu for a family of four? Yeah, that's a little post-breakfast snack for me!). But I'll meddlesomely come down and tell you that a real indulgent pudding is one that puts you to sleep on a dreary winter's afternoon. You've had a big meal, possibly requiring you have a rest before you even think about shovelling more food in, but somehow your pudding stomach still has space, and an indulgent pudding just slides right in!

Here I've tried to focus on a mixture of bakes that are most popular on the market stall – traditional flavour combinations baked a new way and well-known bakes in new flavours. I also wanted to give you a few puddings you can whip up in no time (both the Baked Cookie Dough on page 157 and the Sour Cherry + Chocolate Gelato Cake on page 171 can be made in advance and thrown together at the last second) for times when you're in a hurry to lie down and take a nap yourself!

You'll also find some summer puddings here – the Raspberry Ombré Cheesecake Cake on page 158 is one of my all-time favourites and makes a stunning centrepiece for a garden party, and the Pistachio Tiramisu on page 152 is a perfect treat (and healthy, because nuts).

Pistachio Tiramisu	152
Baked Cookie Dough	157
Raspberry Ombré Cheesecake Cake	158
Baileys Custard Tart	162
Apple Crumble + Custard Cheesecake	165
Biscoff Poke Cake	166
Triple Chocolate Brownie Cake	167
Sour Cherry + Chocolate Gelato Cake	171
Snickers Cake	173

PISTACHIO TIRAMISU

Picture this: you've just worked 137 hours in seven days across a bakery, a photoshoot and a market and have the final day of your photoshoot to go, but you've forgotten to make your pistachio tiramisu. It's 11pm and you have a trifle bowl you need to justify purchasing, the drive to make the best-looking thing yet and *Brooklyn* playing on the TV. That was the situation that led me to make this pistachio tirami-trifle, which is my absolute favourite thing in the entire book! A week later, I'm still eating it, by the spoon, out of the trifle bowl. Photographed is actually double the recipe below but at least now you know it's scalable!

Prep + baking time:
1 hour, plus chilling
Serves: 6

For the sponge fingers:
6 eggs, separated
150g (5¼oz) caster sugar
½ tsp vanilla bean paste
250g (9oz) plain flour
50g (2oz) granulated sugar (optional)

For the coffee soak:
1 tbsp instant coffee
250ml (8½fl oz) water

For the pistachio layers:
500g (1lb 2oz) mascarpone
50ml (2fl oz) pistachio liqueur
300g (10½oz) pistachio cream

To decorate:
75g pistachios, chopped or blitzed

1. Preheat the oven to 180°C/160°C fan/350°F/Gas 4 and line three large baking trays with baking parchment.

2. To make the sponge fingers, whisk the egg whites on a medium-high speed to soft peaks. Slowly add the caster sugar, whisking to incorporate after each addition, until stiff peaks form.

3. Add the egg yolks and vanilla and whisk to combine (this won't take long!), then sift in the flour and whisk again, ensuring all the flour from the bottom is incorporated.

4. Spoon the sponge mixture into a piping bag and cut a large hole, about 2.5cm (1in) wide, in the end. Pipe around 30 sponge fingers, roughly 10cm (4in) long, onto the lined baking trays. Sprinkle the granulated sugar over the biscuits (if using), then bake for 12–14 minutes until golden. Leave to cool.

5. Once the biscuits have cooled, brew the coffee for the soak.

6. To make the pistachio layers, whisk the mascarpone until thick then add the pistachio liqueur and whisk again to combine.

7. Spread a third of the pistachio cream evenly across the bottom of a 2 litre (3½ pint) serving dish. Dunk half of the sponge fingers in the coffee, one at a time, then lay them over the pistachio cream. Spoon half of the mascarpone over and even out with a spoon.

8. Top with another third of the pistachio cream then dunk the remaining sponge fingers in the coffee and arrange them in the dish. Spoon over the remaining mascarpone and again even out with a spoon, then finish with the final third of the pistachio cream.

9. Sprinkle over the pistachios, cover with cling film and refrigerate for at least 2 hours before serving.

GEORGE LOVES A TIP!

— If you're short on time, sub out the homemade sponge fingers for shop-bought ones – ain't no shame in a lazy hack…

— Sprinkling granulated sugar over the sponge fingers is optional – I tend to omit it as the dessert is sweet enough already, but in case there's any left over, adding the sugar will make sure they're sweet enough for you to enjoy on their own.

— You can make this tiramisu up to two days ahead of time and store, covered, in the fridge until ready to serve.

— While you still want the coffee taste to come through, be careful not to brew coffee that is too strong or it will take away from the pistachio flavour – the ratio here is just right!

BAKED COOKIE DOUGH

I see an epidemic online of people baking cookie dough in foil trays, slapping chocolate sauces on top, chucking on a couple of chocolate bars and sending it out on the backs of bicycles for late-night munchie treats. Is this my vibe? Not necessarily, however, I am a man of the people, so here's the best baked cookie dough you'll ever have in your life. The best thing about this recipe is that it's a single (although still quite indulgent) portion! That said, you can easily scale this up. This recipe is somewhere between a traditional baked cookie and an edible cookie dough. It won't crisp up to the point where it's crunchy around the edges, but it absolutely must be baked due to the egg yolks which keep it rich and creamy inside.

Prep + baking time: 20 minutes
Serves: 1

50g (2oz) butter
65g (2½oz) light brown sugar
1 egg yolk
60g (2¼oz) plain flour
¼ tsp baking powder
50g (2oz) chocolate of your choice, chopped
¼ tsp salt flakes
¼ tsp vanilla bean paste

1. Preheat the oven to 180°C/160°C fan/350°F/Gas 4.
2. Cream the butter and sugar together for at least 3 minutes until really creamy, then add the egg yolk, flour and baking powder and mix to form a dough.
3. Add the chocolate and mix to incorporate then tip the mixture into a foil container 15x13cm (6x5in) – they're the standard size smaller ones you can get from supermarkets/get your pilau rice in), sprinkle with the salt and bake for 14 minutes. Cook until the edges are starting to go golden and crisp but the middle is still pale, with a slight crust forming.
4. Leave to stand for 5 minutes (to avoid burning your mouth).
5. Serve with a dollop of ice cream.

GEORGE LOVES A TIP!

— These are easy to make in the air fryer! Just cook at 170°C (325°F) for 8 minutes, leaving to stand for 4 minutes, then tuck in!

— I was all about making this a single portion, but, as you can see from the picture on the cover, we decided to make a giant version in a 26cm (10in) skillet that's five times the regular recipe for the photoshoot and then we all overindulged in the leftovers! It'll take 25 minutes to cook at 180°C/160°C fan/350°F/Gas 4 and the quantities to make this are: 250g (9oz) butter, 325g (11oz) light brown sugar, 5 egg yolks, 300g (10oz) plain flour, 2 tsp baking powder, 250g (9oz) chocolate, 1 tsp salt flakes and 1 tsp vanilla bean paste.

RASPBERRY OMBRÉ CHEESECAKE CAKE

Prep + baking time:
2 hours, plus cooling
Serves: 14

This is hands down the best cake I've come up with in the past couple of years. The cake is incredibly moist and delicate, and the cheesecake is soft with a light raspberry flavour coming through and bringing it all together.

For the sponge:
450g (1lb) butter
450g (1lb) caster sugar
9 eggs
450g (1lb) self-raising flour
2¼ tsp baking powder
1 tsp vanilla bean paste
Pink food colouring, as desired

For the vanilla buttercream:
500g (1lb 2oz) butter
1kg (2lb 3oz) icing sugar
½ tsp vanilla bean paste

For the cheesecake filling:
450g (1lb) cream cheese
75g (2¾oz) icing sugar
200ml (6¾fl oz) double cream
50g (2oz) raspberries

For the ombré buttercream:
200g (7oz) butter
400g (14oz) icing sugar
Pink food colouring, as desired

To decorate:
250g (9oz) raspberries

1. Preheat the oven to 180°C/160°C fan/350°F/Gas 4. Grease and line four 20cm (8in) cake tins.

2. To make the sponge, cream the butter and sugar together for 3–5 minutes until light and fluffy. Add the eggs, flour, baking powder and vanilla and mix to form a batter.

3. Weigh the batter then transfer a quarter to the first cake tin. Add a small drop of pink food colouring to the remaining batter and stir until pale pink, then transfer another quarter to the second cake tin. Add a further few drops of pink food colouring and stir until a slightly darker shade of pink, then transfer another quarter to the third cake tin. Make an even darker shade of pink with the final quarter of the batter and transfer this to the fourth cake tin, then bake all four sponges for 18–22 minutes until a skewer comes out clean. Allow the sponges to cool.

4. Meanwhile, make the vanilla buttercream. Beat the butter until pale and creamy then add the icing sugar and vanilla and beat again until smooth. Set aside.

5. To make the cheesecake filling, whisk the cream cheese, icing sugar and cream together for 3–5 minutes until thick. Push the raspberries through a sieve over a bowl to catch the juice, then fold the juice into the cheesecake mixture – it may seem a little sloppy, but it will firm up as it sets.

6. To assemble, level the sponges using a serrated knife (you can get special wire cutters and levellers for cakes if you're feeling fancy). Dollop and smooth around three quarters of the buttercream over the tops of the three pink sponges then spoon around half of the remainder into a piping bag (setting aside the leftover buttercream to coat the cakes later). Snip a hole roughly 2cm (¾in) in the end of the piping bag and pipe dams of buttercream around the edges of the three iced sponges. Repeat until the buttercream dams are about 2.5cm (1in) high. Fill each crater with a third of the cheesecake mixture and smooth out so the surface is in line with the buttercream walls.

7. Stack the pink sponges on top of each other, darkest to lightest, then top with the uncoloured cake. Wrap the cake in cling film and refrigerate for at least an hour to set.

8. Once the cake has firmed up, coat with the remaining buttercream and smooth, then refrigerate again for 20 minutes. The cake will remain moist as the buttercream creates a seal.

Recipe continues on page 161

Indulgent Puddings

9. To make the ombré buttercream, beat the butter until pale and creamy then add the icing sugar and beat again until smooth. Remove around a fifth of the buttercream and set aside. Add a drop of pink food colouring to the remaining buttercream, mix to combine then remove another fifth and set aside. Repeat with the remaining buttercream to give you one white buttercream and four buttercreams in varying shades of pink.

10. Cover the bottom fifth of the cake with the darkest shade of buttercream, smoothing with a cake scraper or palette knife, then cover the next fifth with the next darkest shade of buttercream. Repeat with the remaining shades of buttercream, finishing with the white buttercream. Run the cake scraper or palette knife under hot water, dry and scrape around the cake to remove any excess buttercream and create an ombré effect. Use any remaining buttercream to cover the top of the cake. Arrange the raspberries on top of the cake and refrigerate until ready to serve.

GEORGE LOVES A TIP!

— Sealing the cake with buttercream helps the sponge to stay moist, so don't worry about having to keep the cake in the fridge – once it's been at room temperature for around an hour it will taste as if it was freshly baked.

— If you fancy whole raspberries in your cheesecake, just fold them through the cheesecake mixture instead of pushing them through a sieve.

BAILEYS CUSTARD TART

This deep, boozy tart is not for the faint hearted! It's the perfect dessert for a special occasion or a cold winter's night, best served with cream or ice cream. It will keep refrigerated in an airtight container for up to five days, if you can resist it for that long. I've also noticed an increasing roster of new 'special edition' Irish cream liqueurs and this recipe will work with most of them, although avoid 'blonde' chocolate-based versions, which are more likely to split the egg custard filling.

Prep + baking time:
1½ hours plus chilling
Serves: 10

For the pastry:
200g (7oz) plain flour, plus extra for dusting
30g (1⅛oz) ground almonds
40g (1½oz) icing sugar
125g (4½oz) cold butter, diced
1 large egg yolk
1 tbsp cold water

For the filling:
12 egg yolks
150g (5¼oz) caster sugar
400ml (13½fl oz) double cream
400ml (13½fl oz) Baileys (or other Irish cream liqueur)

1. To make the pastry, pulse the flour, ground almonds and icing sugar in a food processor until incorporated. Add the butter and egg yolk and pulse until combined, trickling the water in as you go to help form a dough, as needed. Tip the dough onto a lightly floured work surface and bring together with your hands, then roll the pastry out to a circle slightly larger than a 24.5cm (9¾in) deep, loose-bottomed tart tin. Use the pastry to line the tin then refrigerate for 30 minutes.

2. Preheat the oven to 210°C/190°C fan/410°F/Gas 6.

3. Cover the pastry base with a sheet of parchment paper and fill with baking beans. Blind bake for 15 minutes before removing the beans and parchment paper, then bake for a further 5 minutes. Remove the pastry base from the oven and set aside. Reduce the oven temperature to 160°C/140°C fan/320°F/Gas 3.

4. To make the filling, whisk the egg yolks and sugar together until pale. Warm the cream in a small saucepan over a medium heat until beginning to steam, then whisk in the egg yolk and sugar mixture.

5. Add the Baileys, whisking until fully incorporated, then transfer the mixture to a jug.

6. Place the pastry case onto a baking tray (to catch any spills) before carefully pouring in the Baileys egg custard mixture. Bake for 40–45 minutes until just a slight wobble on top remains.

7. Leave to cool completely for about an hour before refrigerating for at least 6 hours. Once set, remove from the tart tin, slice and serve.

GEORGE LOVES A TIP!

— If you want the tart to be less boozy, reduce the Baileys by 100ml (3½fl oz) and substitute for more cream.

— Allow the tart to cool at room temperature before it chills as it will continue to cook as it sets. Refrigerating after cooling helps to create a silky texture.

APPLE CRUMBLE + CUSTARD CHEESECAKE

Prep + baking time:
1 hour, plus chilling
Serves: 8

A crisp, oaty and nutty crumble topped with cinnamon-stewed apples, a custard cheesecake and even more creaminess and crumble on top!

For the apples:
3 Bramley apples, peeled, cored and sliced into 2cm (¾in) chunks
1 tsp cinnamon

For the crumble base:
200g (7oz) plain flour
200g (7oz) light brown sugar
120g (4½oz) butter
35g (1¼oz) oats
15g (½oz) flaked almonds, chopped
15g (½oz) blanched hazelnuts, chopped

For the cheesecake:
90g (3¼oz) Rich Custard (see page 29), plus extra to serve
450g (1lb) cream cheese
300ml (10fl oz) double cream
100g (3½oz) icing sugar

1. Preheat the oven to 180°C/160°C fan/350°F/Gas 4. Grease and line a 20cm (8in) round cake tin.

2. To stew the apples, place the apples, cinnamon and a splash of water in a small saucepan with a lid. Cover the pan and cook over a low heat for 30 minutes, stirring occasionally, until a knife easily cuts through the apples and they're starting to break down. Set aside to cool.

3. Meanwhile, make the crumble. Tip the flour and sugar into a mixing bowl and toss to combine. Rub in the butter until the mixture resembles fine breadcrumbs, then add the oats, almonds and hazelnuts and toss to combine.

4. Tip three quarters of the crumble mixture into the lined cake tin, pushing it down gently to compress. Bake for 15 minutes then leave to cool.

5. Sprinkle the remaining crumble mixture onto a baking tray and bake for 12 minutes until golden on top. Leave to cool.

6. To make the cheesecake, prepare the Rich Custard following the method on page 29 and leave to cool.

7. Whisk together the cream cheese, cream and icing sugar until thick, then add the cooled custard and fold until incorporated.

8. Spoon the stewed apples into the cake tin on top of the crumble base. Top with the cheesecake mixture and level out, then refrigerate for at least 6 hours.

9. When ready to serve, sprinkle over the remaining crumble and serve with my Rich Custard for pouring.

GEORGE LOVES A TIP!
— The longer this is left to set, the more juices will ooze from the freshly stewed apples in the middle layer, so this cheesecake is best made on the morning of the day you plan to serve it.

Indulgent Puddings

BISCOFF POKE CAKE

Prep + baking time:
1 hour
Serves: 8

This is like a milky and fluffy tres leches cake that's been saturated with Biscoff spread, because why not make it even more indulgent?! I use smooth Biscoff spread just because I like the melt-in-your-mouth feeling, but go with the crunchy version and some crushed biscuits on top if you want more texture.

For the cake:
50g (2oz) Biscoff spread
250g (9oz) caster sugar
250g (9oz) double cream
5 eggs, separated
250g (9oz) self-raising flour
1 tsp baking powder

For the topping:
200g (7oz) condensed milk
75g (2¾oz) Biscoff spread
50ml (2fl oz) whole milk

1. Preheat the oven to 180°C/160°C fan/350°F/Gas 4. Grease and line a 25cm (10in) square cake tin.

2. To make the cake, cream the Biscoff spread, caster sugar and cream together until light and fluffy, then add the egg yolks, flour and baking powder and mix to form a thick batter.

3. In a separate bowl, whisk the egg whites to stiff peaks then fold into the batter. Pour into the tin and bake for 32 minutes.

4. Meanwhile, make the topping. Heat the condensed milk and Biscoff spread in a saucepan over a low heat, then add the milk and stir to combine.

5. As soon as the cake leaves the oven, poke holes across the surface and tease the parchment paper away from the sides.

6. Pour two thirds of the Biscoff milk mixture over the cake while it's still in the tin and allow to seep in for 5 minutes, then douse with the remaining third. Leave to cool before serving.

TRIPLE CHOCOLATE BROWNIE CAKE

Prep + baking time:
1½ hours plus chilling
Serves: 12

This is literally just brownies stacked up with three types of chocolate ganache, but boy is it a delicious and amazingly indulgent dessert!

For the brownie rounds:
500g (1lb 2oz) butter
400g (14oz) dark chocolate, broken into pieces
8 eggs
550g (1lb 3oz) golden caster sugar
1 tsp vanilla bean paste
130g (4¾oz) plain flour
160g (5½oz) cocoa powder
1 tsp salt flakes

For the ganaches:
250g (9oz) dark chocolate, broken into pieces
250g (9oz) milk chocolate, broken into pieces
250g (9oz) white chocolate, broken into pieces
450ml (15fl oz) double cream

1. Preheat the oven to 180°C/160°C fan/350°F/Gas 4. Grease and line four 20cm (8in) round cake tins.

2. To make the brownies, melt the butter and dark chocolate together in a bowl over a bain-marie, stirring until smooth, then set aside to cool slightly.

3. In a separate bowl whisk the eggs, vanilla bean paste and sugar together until thick, pale and doubled in size. Pour the melted chocolate into the egg mixture and whisk until just combined. Sieve in the flour and cocoa powder, sprinkle with the salt and fold to a smooth batter.

4. Divide the batter between the four cake tins and bake for 22–26 minutes until there's just a slight wobble on top, or when a thermometer reads 89°C (192°F). Leave to cool at room temperature for 10 minutes before refrigerating for at least 6 hours, preferably overnight.

5. When set, make the three ganaches, starting with the white chocolate as this tends to take longer to set (see tip, below). Melt the white chocolate in a bowl over a bain-marie, stirring until smooth. Add 150ml (5¼fl oz) of the cream, whisk to combine, then set aside. Use the same method to make the milk chocolate and dark chocolate ganaches.

6. Spoon the milk chocolate ganache into a piping bag, snip off the end and pipe a dam of ganache around the edges of three of the brownie rounds, reserving three quarters of the ganache. Fill the second piping bag with the white chocolate ganache, reserving one quarter of the mixture, snip off the end and fill the milk chocolate ganache wells with the white chocolate ganache, reserving a fifth of the mixture.

Recipe continues on page 168

7. Stack the brownie rounds on top of each other, finishing with the fourth undecorated round. Refrigerate for 10 minutes to firm up (this'll happen very fast!).

8. Coat the chilled brownie stack with the dark chocolate ganache, reserving a little for decorating, then return to the fridge for a further 10 minutes. Spoon the remaining dark chocolate ganache into a piping bag and snip off the end.

9. Starting at the bottom, pipe lines of each ganache around the cake, from dark to white chocolate, before smoothing with a cake scraper. Use any remaining ganache to decorate the top of the cake.

GEORGE LOVES A TIP!

— The ganaches need to be at a pipeable consistency when icing the cake. White chocolate ganache often needs a little longer to reach that than milk and dark chocolate, so make this first while you make the others.

SOUR CHERRY + CHOCOLATE GELATO CAKE

Prep + baking time:
1½ hours, plus freezing overnight
Serves: 8

Sour cherries are the closest thing to sour sweets you can get in dried fruit form – the flavour is sharp, sweet and sour and they're highly addictive! I only discovered sour cherry molasses about six months ago and have been using it instead of balsamic vinegar on burrata toast all summer, but it's also great in desserts when balanced correctly! If you're making the gelato using an ice cream machine with a bowl that needs to be frozen, make sure you get it in the freezer the night before making this.

For the gelato:
4 egg yolks
150g (5¼oz) caster sugar
150ml (5¼fl oz) milk
350ml (12fl oz) double cream
1 tsp vanilla bean paste
75g (2¾oz) dried sour cherries
150g (5¼oz) dark chocolate, finely chopped
50ml (2fl oz) sour cherry molasses

For the sponge:
3 eggs plus 3 whites
100g (3½oz) ground almonds
110g (3¾oz) caster sugar
20g (¾oz) cocoa powder
40g (1½oz) plain flour
25g (1oz) butter, melted

For the coating:
250g (9oz) mascarpone
100ml (3½fl oz) double cream
1 tbsp sour cherry molasses
Cocoa powder, for dusting

1. If needed, remember to put the bowl of your ice cream machine into the freezer!

2. To make the gelato, line two 900g (2lb) loaf tins with cling film. Whisk the egg yolks with 75g (2¾oz) of the sugar until pale, thick and creamy. Set aside.

3. Heat the remaining sugar, milk, 150ml (5¼fl oz) of the cream and the vanilla in a medium saucepan over a medium heat, whisking until starting to steam.

4. Re-whisk the egg yolks and sugar then pour into the pan with the cream mixture and whisk until thick and steaming. Add the remaining cream, whisking as you go.

5. Pour the gelato mixture into your ice cream machine and leave to churn for 30 minutes until cooled, then add the sour cherries and dark chocolate and continue to churn for 2 hours until thickened.

6. Decant the gelato into the lined loaf tins. Drizzle over the molasses and use a skewer to ripple through the mixture. Freeze overnight until set.

7. Preheat the oven to 180°C/160°C fan/350°F/Gas 4. Grease and line a 20x30cm swiss roll tin.

8. To make the sponge, whisk the whole eggs, ground almonds and sugar together until pale and thick. In a separate bowl, whisk the egg whites to soft peaks.

9. Use a clean spatula to fold a quarter of the egg whites into the almond and sugar mixture to loosen. Sieve in the cocoa powder and flour, add the remaining egg whites and melted butter and fold to a smooth batter.

Recipe continues on page 172

Indulgent Puddings

10. Pour into the lined cake tin and bake for 12–15 minutes until a skewer comes out clean. Leave to cool.

11. Meanwhile, make the coating. Whisk the mascarpone and cream together until thick. Add the molasses and whisk to combine.

12. Remove the gelato from the freezer and decant from the tins. Slice the sponge into 3, to form three 20cm x 10cm strips and place the gelato between the layers, trimming any excess if needed. Coat the cake with the mascarpone and dust with sieved cocoa powder.

> **GEORGE LOVES A TIP!**
>
> — Store the cake in the fridge before serving – it won't dry the cake at all as it's sealed in with the ganache and the nougat and caramel will help to keep it moist!
>
> — Don't be tempted to dollop and spread the nougat onto the sponges rather than piping – it will pull the sponge apart and cause a crumbly catastrophe. Instead, pipe the nougat on and smush it down with the next sponge layer to keep the cake even and level.

SNICKERS CAKE

Prep + baking time:
1½ hours, plus cooling
Serves: 10

This is a moisterpiece if ever I did see one. Just don't make it if you're allergic to peanuts, for obvious reasons…

For the sponge:
6 eggs plus 6 whites
200g (7oz) ground almonds
250g (9oz) caster sugar
80g (3oz) plain flour
40g (1½oz) cocoa powder
50g (2oz) butter, melted

For the nougat:
250g (9oz) caster sugar
150g (5¼oz) honey
22g (¾oz) liquid glucose
125ml (4¼fl oz) water
2 egg whites (approx. 80g/3oz)

For the peanut caramel:
250g (9oz) Thiccc Caramel (see page 22)
30g (1oz) roasted, salted peanuts, chopped, plus extra to decorate

For the ganache:
300g (10½oz) dark chocolate, broken into pieces
150ml (5¼fl oz) double cream

1. Preheat the oven to 180°C/160°C fan/350°F/Gas 4. Grease and line six 20cm (8in) round cakes tins.

2. To make the sponge, whisk the whole eggs, ground almonds and sugar together until pale, creamy and doubled in size, then set aside.

3. In a separate bowl, whisk the egg whites to soft peaks. Use a clean spatula to fold a quarter of the egg whites into the yolk mixture to loosen, then fold through the remaining egg whites. Sieve in the flour and cocoa powder, then add the melted butter by gently pouring it against the side of the bowl so as not to knock any air out of the batter. Fold to a lump-free batter.

4. Divide the mixture between the six lined cake tins and baked for 11–13 minutes until a skewer comes out clean. Set aside to cool.

5. To make the nougat, heat the sugar, honey, liquid glucose and water in a medium saucepan over a medium heat until the sugar has dissolved and formed a syrup. Turn the heat up to high and bring to the boil – you eventually want the mixture to reach 160°C (320°F).

6. When the syrup reaches 145°C (300°F), begin whisking the egg whites to form soft peaks. When the syrup reaches 160°C (320°F), slowly pour the syrup into the egg whites with the whisk on high speed until the mixture begins to thicken. Slowly reduce the speed of the whisk as the nougat thickens and cools down. This should take 3–5 minutes.

7. To make the peanut caramel, prepare the Thiccc Caramel following the method on page 22 then stir in the peanuts.

8. To assemble, scrape the nougat into a piping bag, snip off the end and pipe onto three of the sponges (see tip, below). Spread the peanut caramel over two of the remaining sponges. Starting with a nougat-topped sponge, stack the sponges on top of each other, alternating the nougat and peanut caramel-covered sponges, then finish with the plain one. Wrap the cake in cling film and refrigerate for at least an hour to firm up.

9. When firm, make the ganache. Melt the chocolate in a bowl over a bain-marie then beat in the double cream until glossy. Allow to set a little until spreadable.

10. Coat the cake in the ganache using a mini palette knife, sprinkle the peanuts around the edge and serve.

Indulgent Puddings

07

COSY FAVOURITES

In a book about comfort, it's hard not to include a few traditional favourites, yet I still had to chuck in some 'George' twists and the bakes I was craving at the time of writing! These recipes all fall into one of those categories – and the Espresso Martini Hot Fudge Brownie Sundae is here on page 179 so I could legitimately eat/drink it, for recipe-testing purposes, to get me through 48 hours of photoshoots over six of the busiest days of the baking year.

Some of the recipes in this chapter have become my new go-tos – I've been making carrot cake for markets purely so I can smuggle a slice home. Treacle tart has long been nestled between cakes in one of my most popular market bakes, so unleashing it and making it gihumungenormous has been a delight. One of the chest freezers at work (kept out of the way and purely for me to hoard my bulk cooking and leftover bakes to cater for my own wake – I'm morbid but efficient) has since become a gelato store. Only two gelato recipes made it into this book (and you can find them on pages 171 and 187) but that hasn't stopped me making enough flavours to fill an entire George's Gelato book!

Also, a note on cornflakes because I get messages about this constantly – the cornflake-based recipe in the Salted Caramel Cornflake Sandwiches on page 192 is the same one I use for all my cornflake delights!

Spotted Dick Traybake	178
Espresso Martini Hot Fudge Brownie Sundae	179
Sticky Toffee Pudding	183
Carrot Cake	184
Chocolate Gelato	187
Treacle Tart	188
Chocolate Fudge Cookies	191
Salted Caramel Cornflake Sandwiches	192
Tahini, Dark Chocolate + Sesame Cookies	195
Chocolate Orange Loaf Cake	196
Plum Crumble Cake	198
Toasted Honey, Pear + Cinnamon Cake	201

SPOTTED DICK TRAYBAKE

I couldn't write a comfort bakes book and not put a spotted dick in it! Despite the rumours, I'd never even tried spotted dick until I decided to put a recipe in this book. Traditionally it's a steamed pudding but I don't have a steamer, so this pudding is baked with a baking tray filled with water beneath it to create a bit of steam in the oven – just don't forget it's filled with water when you remove it later on!

Prep + baking time:
1½ hours
Serves: 6

For the traybake:
150g (5¼oz) currants
100ml (3½fl oz) boiling water
300g (10½oz) self-raising flour
1 tsp salt
100g (3½oz) suet
85g (3oz) caster sugar
Zest of 2 lemons
225ml (7½fl oz) whole milk

To serve:
1 quantity of Rich Custard (see page 29)

1. Preheat the oven to 140°C/120°C fan/275°F/Gas 1. Grease and line a 20cm (8in) square cake tin. Place a deep grill pan, baking tray or roasting dish in the bottom of the oven and use a jug to half fill it with water.

2. Tip the currants into a bowl, pour over the boiling water and set aside for 5 minutes.

3. Meanwhile, combine the flour, salt, suet, sugar and lemon zest together in a mixing bowl.

4. Drain the water from the currants and add the currants to the dry mixture. Pour in the milk and bring the mixture together to form a dough.

5. Transfer the dough to the lined tin and cover with foil.

6. Cook the pudding on the middle shelf of the oven for 1 hour until a skewer comes out clean. Serve with my Rich Custard (see page 29)!

ESPRESSO MARTINI HOT FUDGE BROWNIE SUNDAES

This one's a real mash-up – the love child of affogato and chocolate fudge sundae with an espresso martini twist! If it were me, I'd be serving this in a champagne coupe, with the sundae balancing precariously in the cocktail glass, catching dripping gelato and boozy cream in a receptacle below. However, good luck constructing that without spilling your cocktail, so just build it inside a knickerbocker glory glass instead!

Prep + baking time:
1 hour
Serves: 2

For the brownie:
200g (7oz) dark chocolate, broken into pieces
250g (9oz) butter
1 tbsp coffee granules, mixed with 25ml (1fl oz) boiling water
4 eggs
250g (9oz) golden caster sugar
80g (3oz) cocoa powder
65g (2½oz) plain flour
1 tsp salt

To assemble:
100g (3½oz) mascarpone
50g (2oz) double cream
15ml (½fl oz) Kahlúa

To serve:
1 quantity of Chocolate Gelato (see page 187)
1 quantity of Chocolate Fudge Sauce (see page 31)
1 shot of espresso

1. Prepare the Chocolate Gelato following the method on page 187.
2. Preheat the oven to 180°C/160°C fan/350°F/Gas 4. Grease and line a 25cm (10in) square cake tin.
3. To make the brownie, melt the chocolate and butter together in a bowl over a bain-marie, add the coffee and stir until smooth, then set aside to cool slightly.
4. Meanwhile, whisk the eggs and sugar together in a separate bowl until thick, frothy and doubled in size.
5. Tip the egg mixture into the cooled melted chocolate mixture and whisk until just incorporated. Sieve in the cocoa powder and flour, sprinkle with the salt and fold to combine.
6. Pour the mixture into the lined cake tin and bake for 22–26 minutes until there's a slight wobble on top, or when a thermometer reads 89°C (192°F).
7. Leave to cool at room temperature for 10 minutes, then refrigerate for at least 4 hours, preferably overnight, to get that perfect fudgy texture.
8. Meanwhile, make the Chocolate Fudge Sauce following the method on page 31.
9. When you're ready to assemble, whisk the mascarpone and cream together until just beginning to thicken, then add the Kahlúa and whisk until thick.
10. Remove the tin from the fridge and slice the brownie to your desired size.
11. Douse your serving glasses in the warm Chocolate Fudge Sauce, reserving a little for drizzling. Add a piece of brownie to each glass and top with a dollop of the Kahlúa cream. Add scoops of Chocolate Gelato, pour over your espresso, drizzle over some more Chocolate Fudge Sauce and enjoy!

STICKY TOFFEE PUDDING

I'm not dumb, I know that the biggest challenge here will probably be convincing you to actually put dates in your sticky toffee pudding. I'm pretty sure the hate stems from the near-universal childhood recollection of biting into a cookie or biscuit, excited to taste those sweet chocolate chips, only to be left in floods of tears as our teeth tore through dry, chewy raisins. But I guarantee that adult you will enjoy dates in this! By soaking them in milk, they become melt-in-your-mouth soft once baked and add lots of flavour.

Prep + baking time:
1½ hours
Serves: 6

For the pudding:
200g (7oz) stoned dates, roughly chopped
250ml (8½fl oz) whole milk
150g (5¼oz) butter
175g (6oz) light brown sugar
25g (1oz) date molasses
25g (1oz) treacle
2 eggs plus 1 yolk
175g (6oz) plain flour
½ tsp baking powder
1 tsp bicarbonate of soda
1 tsp vanilla bean paste
½ tsp salt

To serve:
1 quantity Sticky Toffee Sauce (see page 26)

1. Preheat the oven to 170°C/150°C fan/325°F/Gas 3. Grease a 1.5l (50fl oz) baking dish or grease and line a 20cm (8in) cake tin (see tip below).

2. Warm the dates and milk in a small saucepan over a medium heat until steaming but not simmering. Remove from the heat and leave to cool.

3. Cream the butter, sugar, date molasses and treacle together until creamy and well incorporated. Add the whole eggs and egg yolk and mix to loosen the mixture.

4. Sieve in the flour, baking powder and bicarbonate of soda and beat to combine, then fold in the vanilla and salt. Finally, pour in the milk and date mixture and fold to a smooth batter.

5. Pour the batter into the lined baking dish and bake for 50 minutes until golden brown on top and a skewer inserted comes out mostly clean.

6. Serve with my Sticky Toffee Sauce (see page 26).

GEORGE LOVES A TIP!

— I'm a firm believer that sticky toffee pudding should be made ahead and reheated before serving. Allowing it to cool and finish cooking in the tin stops the top of the pudding forming too much of crust. Simply microwave in portions or cover the tray with foil and warm through in the oven to get it hot before dousing in Sticky Toffee Sauce and enjoying!

— For a deeper pudding use a 20cm (8in) cake tin lined with untrimmed parchment paper.

CARROT CAKE

This is about as classic as I feel I can go in a cookbook without giving a recipe nobody will bother making because everyone already has their favourite. There are dense carrot cakes and fluffy ones, and this is on the fluffier side, so I'd consider it more of a summer recipe. I recently discovered that some people don't peel their carrots before grating them when making a carrot cake – I'm here to tell you that's vile and should be a criminal offence. Let's maintain some decorum OMG!

Prep + baking time: 1 hour, plus cooling
Serves: 8

For the sponge:
250g (9oz) light brown sugar
200ml (6¾fl oz) vegetable oil
4 eggs plus 2 yolks
250g (9oz) plain flour
3 tsp baking powder
½ tsp bicarbonate of soda
1 tsp cinnamon
¼ tsp ground cloves
¼ tsp ground nutmeg
300g (10½oz) carrots, peeled and grated
75g (2¾oz) walnuts
50g (2oz) pecans
100g (3½oz) raisins

For the icing:
180g (5½oz) butter
120g (4½oz) cream cheese
600g (1lb 5oz) icing sugar
½ tsp vanilla bean paste

1. Preheat the oven to 180°C/160°C fan/350°F/Gas 4 and line three 20cm (8in) round cake tins.

2. To make the sponge, place the sugar, oil, eggs and egg yolks into a mixing bowl and whisk for 3–5 minutes until doubled in size, pale and frothy. Add the flour, baking powder, bicarbonate of soda and spices and fold through until smooth.

3. Add the carrots, walnuts, pecans and raisins and fold to combine. Divide the mixture equally between the three lined tins and bake for 30 minutes until a skewer comes out clean. Leave to cool.

4. Meanwhile, make the icing. Cream the butter, cream cheese and icing sugar together until smooth. Add the vanilla and stir well to combine.

5. To assemble, level the sponges with a serrated knife. Spread half of the icing over two of the sponges, then stack them on top of each other, followed by the un-iced sponge. Use the second half of the icing to coat the sides and top of the cake before decorating as fancy as you like and enjoying!

GEORGE LOVES A TIP!

— I won't claim it as my own, but I once read a Mary Berry carrot cake recipe where she used a tablespoon of orange curd in the frosting which is a stroke of genius! I like to keep it simple but if you want to mix it up a little, this would be my recommended method.

CHOCOLATE GELATO

Homemade gelato tastes incredible and is perfect with so many desserts – cookies, brownies, puddings, the list goes on... The easiest way to make gelato is to buy a cheap ice cream machine with a freezable bowl to pour your mixture straight into – this way you'll be able to scoop it within a couple of hours of churning! The richness of this gelato depends on the quality of your ingredients – using high percentage cocoa powder and chocolate will give an extremely indulgent dessert, so don't be tempted to skimp too much!

Prep time:
30 minutes, plus freezing and churning
Serves: 6

4 egg yolks
150g (5¼oz) caster sugar
50g (2oz) cocoa powder
150ml (5¼fl oz) whole milk
350ml (12fl oz) double cream
150g (5¼oz) dark chocolate, broken into pieces

1. Pop the bowl of your ice cream machine into the freezer (referring to the manufacturer's instructions).

2. Whisk the egg yolks with 75g (2¾oz) of the sugar until thick and creamy, then set aside.

3. Heat the cocoa powder, remaining sugar, milk and 150ml (5¼fl oz) of the cream in a medium saucepan over a medium heat, whisking together until the cocoa powder and sugar have dissolved and the mixture has started to steam.

4. Add the chocolate and whisk until melted.

5. Re-whisk the egg yolks and sugar, pour into the pan and whisk until thick and well combined, then add the remaining cream, whisking as you go.

6. Pour the gelato mixture into your ice cream machine and wait for a couple of hours until thick and frozen. Decant into a tub and stash in the freezer.

GEORGE LOVES A TIP!

— To make vanilla gelato, omit the cocoa powder and chocolate and up the amount of double cream to 450ml (15fl oz). Follow the recipe as above, adding 10g (¼oz) vanilla bean paste before decanting into the ice cream maker.

TREACLE TART

I don't think many people realize treacle tart is just breadcrumbs soaked in golden syrup and baked until juuuust set. For such basic ingredients it's one of the most indulgent puddings going and is perfect for a cold autumn/winter's day. Don't be tempted to keep peeking into the oven to check how the cooking is going, just let it work its magic!

Prep + baking time: 2 hours, plus chilling
Serves: 12

For the pastry:
200g (7oz) plain flour, plus extra for dusting
30g (1⅛oz) ground almonds
40g (1½oz) icing sugar
125g (4½oz) cold butter, diced
1 large egg yolk
1 tbsp cold water

For the filling:
700g (1lb 9oz) white bread, crusts removed
100ml (3½fl oz) whole milk
4 eggs
1.3kg (3lb) golden syrup
Juice of 1 lemon

1. To make the pastry, pulse the flour, ground almonds and icing sugar in a food processor until incorporated. Add the butter and egg yolk and pulse until combined, trickling the water in as you go to help form a dough. Tip the dough onto a lightly floured work surface and bring together with your hands, then roll the pastry out to a circle slightly larger than a 24.5cm (9¾in) tart tin. Use the pastry to line the tin then refrigerate for 30 minutes.

2. Preheat the oven to 210°C/190°C fan/410°F/Gas 6.

3. Line the chilled pastry case with parchment paper and fill with baking beans. Bake for 15 minutes, then remove the baking beans and bake for a further 5 minutes. Remove from the oven and reduce the oven temperature to 160°C/140°C fan/320°F/Gas 3.

4. To make the filling, blitz the bread into breadcrumbs and set aside.

5. Whisk the milk and eggs together in a mixing bowl, then add the golden syrup and lemon juice and fold through until smooth.

6. Fold the breadcrumbs into the milk and egg mixture and leave to soak for 10 minutes.

7. Place the pastry case onto a baking tray (to catch any spillages), pour the breadcrumb mixture into the case and bake for 90 minutes until golden on top with a slight wobble in the middle. Allow to cool before removing from the tin, slicing and serving.

GEORGE LOVES A TIP!

— You might be thinking that the cooking time is too long and the oven temperature is too low, but trust the process with this one! You can allow it to set and cool completely before serving as it'll continue cooking in the tin. It can then be reheated and served with ice cream.

Cosy Favourites

CHOCOLATE FUDGE COOKIES

Prep + baking time:
45 minutes, plus chilling
Serves: 8

These cookies are a revelation! Think a brownie in cookie form, with crispy cracked tops and fudgy centres. One of the main secrets here is setting them in the fridge for at least 30 minutes, which gives them an extra-gooey melt-in-the-mouth texture.

135g (4¾oz) butter
175g (6oz) dark chocolate, finely chopped
40g (1½oz) cocoa powder
2 eggs plus 1 yolk
125g (4½oz) light brown sugar
100g (3½oz) caster sugar
100g (3½oz) plain flour
1 tsp salt flakes
100g (3½oz) milk chocolate chips

1. Preheat the oven to 190°C/170°C fan/375°F/Gas 5 and line two large baking trays.

2. Melt the butter in a saucepan over a medium-high heat for 3–5 minutes until frothy and beginning to turn brown.

3. Add the dark chocolate and cocoa powder and stir until melted and smooth. Remove from the heat and set aside.

4. In a separate bowl, whisk together the eggs, egg yolk and sugars until thick and pale. Add the melted chocolate and butter mixture and stir until combined.

5. Fold in the flour, salt and chocolate chips until well incorporated then use a scoop or spoons to dollop eight cookie-shapes onto the lined baking trays, ensuring they're evenly distributed to allow space for them to spread. Bake for 12 minutes until cracked on top.

6. Leave to cool for 5 minutes before placing the trays in the fridge for at least 30 minutes.

GEORGE LOVES A TIP!

— If you want to enjoy these cookies warm, give them a short blast in the microwave or oven to heat them through again. Serve with a dollop of ice cream for an extra comfort hit.

— You can make a glaze for these cookies by sieving 30g (1⅛oz) of icing sugar and 30g (1⅛oz) of cocoa powder into a bowl. Slowly pour in 60ml (2¼oz) of whole milk, stirring as you go, to form a thick glaze. Spoon the glaze over the cookies and pop them back into the fridge to set until you're ready to enjoy them.

SALTED CARAMEL CORNFLAKE SANDWICHES

Ever since I created the Salted Caramel Cornflake Crevice for *Rebel Bakes*, people haven't been able to get enough of salted caramel cornflakes in any form possible! This incarnation uses rounds of the mixture to sandwich chocolate ganache with my Creamy Caramel (see page 21). Every time I've posted videos of us slicing into this, in all its ASMR glory, it's gone viral online and we've struggled to make enough to keep up with demand! You lovely lot enjoy them so much that we've created multiple different flavours, all with the same core recipe, that I hope you can have some fun with!

Prep + baking time:
1 hour, plus chilling
Serves: 7–8

For the cornflake rounds:
200g (7oz) milk chocolate, broken into pieces
100g (3½oz) mini marshmallows
900g (2lb) Salted Caramel (see page 23)
700g (1lb 9oz) cornflakes

For the filling:
½ quantity of Creamy Caramel (see page 21)

For the ganache:
500g (1lb 2oz) dark chocolate, broken into pieces
300ml (10fl oz) double cream

1. To make the cornflake rounds, heat the chocolate, marshmallows and salted caramel together in a large saucepan over a low heat, stirring occasionally, until the marshmallows have almost melted.

2. Remove the pan from the heat and beat until the marshmallows have completely dissolved and the mixture has increased in volume.

3. Add half of the cornflakes and stir to coat in the caramel mixture. Add the remaining cornflakes and continue to stir until completely coated in the caramallow concoction. Allow to cool for around 15 minutes until cool enough to handle.

4. Meanwhile, line a large baking sheet with parchment paper.

5. Use a burger press to create the cornflake rounds. Dollop a couple of tablespoons of the cornflake mixture into a burger press and squash down to create an even disc. Decant onto the lined baking sheet and repeat to create 14 rounds. Cover and refrigerate for at least 2 hours.

6. Meanwhile, make the Creamy Caramel following the method on page 21.

7. When you're ready to assemble, make the ganache. Melt the chocolate in a large bowl over a bain-marie, stirring until smooth and leave to cool. Add the cream, straight from the fridge, and beat to form a thick ganache.

8. Spoon into a piping bag fitted with your choice of nozzle and pipe a circle of ganache around the edge of seven of the cornflake rounds. Fill the centres with the Creamy Caramel before sandwiching with a second cornflake round. Keep refrigerated until ready to consume!

GEORGE LOVES A TIP!

— Keep the cornflake rounds in an airtight container in the fridge so they don't go soggy.

— Pipe the ganache and sandwich the cornflake rounds fast – as soon as the ganache hits the cold cornflake rounds it will begin to set, making it harder to stick the rounds together.

Cosy Favourites

TAHINI, DARK CHOCOLATE + SESAME COOKIES

Prep + baking time: 30 minutes
Serves: 10

These cookies aren't quite as sweet as my others and have a much deeper, more complex flavour. I like to use an 85 per cent cocoa dark chocolate to make them a little bitter.

160g (5½oz) butter
25g (1oz) tahini
1 tbsp date molasses
100g (3½oz) light brown sugar
75g (2¾oz) caster sugar
250g (9oz) plain flour
2 egg yolks
½ tsp salt flakes
½ tsp baking powder
¼ tsp bicarbonate of soda
150g (5¼oz) dark chocolate, chopped into chunks
35g (1¼oz) sesame seeds

1. Preheat the oven to 190°C/170°C fan/375°F/Gas 5 and line two large baking sheets.

2. Melt the butter in a saucepan over a medium-high heat for 3–5 minutes until frothy and beginning to turn brown. Remove from the heat and allow to cool slightly.

3. Add the tahini and molasses to the cooled butter and stir until well combined.

4. Tip the sugars into a mixing bowl and pour over the melted butter mixture. Stir well until the sugar has dissolved. Add the flour, egg yolks, salt, baking powder and bicarbonate of soda and beat to form a dough. Add the chocolate and stir until evenly distributed.

5. Tip the sesame seeds into a bowl. Weigh the dough and divide into ten equal portions, then roll each portion into a ball. Roll each dough ball in the sesame seeds until evenly coated, place on the lined baking sheets and bake for 10–12 minutes until golden and the sesame seeds are toasted.

GEORGE LOVES A TIP!

— Let it be known, these are probably the ugliest cookies I have ever made, but the flavour is so good that I didn't want to tweak the recipe for aesthetic purposes! If you're after less of a mound and more of a round, flat cookie, gently push the cookie dough down onto the baking sheet before cooking.

CHOCOLATE ORANGE LOAF CAKE

I used to receive a Terry's Chocolate Orange from my godmother every Christmas and it quickly turned into my favourite chocolate because there was no guilt eating half of it for breakfast before tucking into my Christmas dinner! This cake encompasses that feeling and really screams breakfast with the addition of the marmalade syrup. Feel free to use orange-flavoured chocolate in the cake if you have some at your disposal, although I prefer a dark chocolate to counteract the sweet syrup.

Prep + baking time:
1½ hours
Serves: 8

For the sponge:
250g (9oz) butter
250g (9oz) caster sugar
5 eggs, beaten
250g (9oz) self-raising flour
200g (7oz) dark chocolate, chopped
1 tbsp plain flour
Zest of 1 orange

For the syrup:
Juice of 1 orange
100g (3½oz) caster sugar
150g (5¼oz) marmalade

For the ganache:
75g (2¾oz) dark chocolate, broken into pieces
75g (2¾oz) double cream

1. Preheat the oven to 180°C/160°C fan/350°F/Gas 4. Grease and line a 900g (2lb) loaf tin.

2. To make the sponge, cream the butter and sugar together until light and fluffy. Gradually add the eggs, beating after each addition, until fully incorporated. Add the self-raising flour and beat again to form a batter. Set aside.

3. In a separate large bowl, toss the dark chocolate with the plain flour to stop it sinking in the cake, then add the orange zest and toss to combine.

4. Add the chocolate and orange zest to the batter and fold to combine, then transfer to the lined tin. Bake for 55–60 minutes until a skewer comes out clean.

5. When the cake has nearly finished baking, make the syrup. Heat the orange juice, sugar and marmalade in a small saucepan over a medium heat, whisking until simmering, reduced and sticky.

6. As soon as the loaf cake is out of the oven, spoon the syrup over the cake in intervals, allowing the syrup to soak in and form a crust after each addition – this will take about 10 minutes. Set aside to cool.

7. To make the ganache, melt the chocolate in a bowl over a bain-marie, stirring until smooth. Add the cream and beat until thickened.

8. Spread the ganache evenly over the top of the cooled cake, then allow to set before slicing up and enjoying.

GEORGE LOVES A TIP!

— You can prick the cake all over before spooning over the syrup for extra stickification.

— I love eating this cake as warm as possible, so I only wait about 30 minutes before adding my ganache to the top, then I leave it to set for about 15 minutes before digging in.

PLUM CRUMBLE CAKE

I love plums! I used to make a delicious plum crumble traybake, but it didn't seem grand enough for this book, so this ginormous beast is here instead. Don't forget to listen to Troye Sivan's 'Plum' as you bake this – I could listen to an entire fruit-based playlist while baking and I'm pretty sure that would count as one of my five-a-day, via osmosis, as a slice of this would.

Prep + baking time:
2 hours, plus cooling
Serves: 16

For the sponge:
450g (1lb) butter
450g (1lb) caster sugar
9 eggs
450g (1lb) self-raising flour
2¼ tsp baking powder
10 drops of custard flavouring

For the plums:
400g (14oz) plums, stoned and diced
2 cloves
1 star anise
50ml (2fl oz) water

For the crumble:
70g (2¾oz) butter
150g (5¼oz) plain flour
80g (3oz) light brown sugar

For the buttercream:
600g (1lb 5oz) butter
1.2kg (2lb 10oz) icing sugar
Custard flavouring, to taste
Purple food colouring, as desired

1. Preheat the oven to 180°C/160°C fan/350°F/Gas 4. Grease and line four 20cm (8in) round cake tins and line a large baking tray.

2. To make the sponge, cream the butter and sugar together until light and fluffy. Add the eggs, flour and baking powder and beat to form a batter. Add the custard flavouring and mix to combine. Divide the batter equally between the lined tins and cook for 18–22 minutes until a skewer comes out clean. Allow the cakes to cool.

3. Meanwhile, place the plums, cloves and star anise in a medium saucepan with a lid. Pour over the water, cover the pan and bring to a simmer over a medium heat. Allow to simmer for 30 minutes until a knife can easily cut through the plums. Set aside to cool.

4. To make the crumble, preheat the oven to 190°C/170°C fan/375°F/Gas 5. Rub the butter into the flour until the mixture resembles coarse breadcrumbs, then add the sugar and stir to combine.

5. Tip the crumble mixture into the lined baking tray and bake for 12–15 minutes until crisp and golden.

6. To make the buttercream, beat the butter until pale and creamy then add the icing sugar and beat again until smooth. Add the custard flavouring to taste and a few drops of purple food colouring and beat until thoroughly incorporated.

7. To assemble, level the tops of the sponges using a serrated knife. Spread buttercream over the tops of three of the sponges, then spoon more buttercream into a piping bag fitted with your favourite nozzle, reserving enough to coat the cake later. Pipe dams of buttercream around the edge of the three sponges.

8. Remove the cloves and star anise from the stewed plums then spoon the plums into the centre of each of the three sponges. Top with the crumble, reserving a little for decorating, then stack the sponges on top of each other, finishing with the plain sponge. Wrap the cake in cling film and refrigerate for 20 minutes to firm up.

9. Remove the cake from the fridge and coat with the remaining buttercream. Decorate with the leftover crumble and serve.

TOASTED HONEY, PEAR + CINNAMON CAKE

This autumnal favourite owes its origins to the glut of pears from a pear tree that grew in the middle of my parents' garden. Here you'll be toasting the honey, which cleverly helps bolster the cheaper versions by making them taste just as good as the expensive kinds (though not the manuka ones that you need to remortgage your house for).

Prep + baking time:
1 hour plus cooling
Serves: 12

For the sponge:
65g (2½oz) honey
300g (10½oz) butter
225g (8oz) caster sugar
6 eggs
300g (10½oz) self-raising flour
1½ tsp baking powder
1 tsp ground cinnamon
200g (7oz) pears, peeled, cored and diced

For the buttercream:
30g (1⅛oz) honey
300g (10½oz) butter
600g (1lb 5oz) icing sugar

1. Preheat the oven to 180°C/160°C fan/350°F/Gas 4. Grease and line three 20cm (8in) round cake tins.

2. To make the sponge, heat the honey in a small saucepan over a low heat for 5 minutes until darkened in colour. Leave to cool.

3. Meanwhile, cream the butter and sugar together until light and fluffy. Add the eggs, flour, baking powder and cinnamon and beat to form a batter.

4. Pour the warmed honey into the batter, add the pears and stir to combine. Pour into the lined tins and bake for 24–26 minutes until golden on top and a skewer comes out clean. Leave to cool.

5. To make the buttercream, heat the honey in a small saucepan over a low heat for 5 minutes as before then set aside to cool slightly. Meanwhile, beat the butter until pale and creamy then add the icing sugar and beat again until smooth.

6. Pour the warm honey into the butter and sugar mixture and stir to combine.

7. To assemble the cake, use a serrated knife to level off the sponges. Use half of the buttercream to stack the sponges on top of each other, then coat the top and sides of the cake with the remaining buttercream.

GEORGE LOVES A TIP!
— This cake can be extremely short and crumbly. To ensure it looks as neat as possible, wrap in cling film and refrigerate for 10 minutes before icing, or crumb coat your cake and then refrigerate.

ACKNOWLEDGEMENTS

Well at least this was easier than the first one!

Thank you so much to my editor Nicole, for believing in my recipes enough to warrant a second book in the first place and for all of your wisdom and guidance. I probably would've been cancelled if you hadn't changed some of my ramblings, and having to listen to all of my voice notes is likely a job in itself.

Thank you to Charlotte for managing everything, helping to keep me on track and being attentive to all of my questions... and ordering the best lunches on shoot!

For the amazing photography once again, thank you so much Kimberly for absolutely nailing the theme and capturing my creations with passion. Thank you also to Katie for again making all of my late-night and manically-made bakes look so incredible! To Rosie, for coming in on our most frantic day and fitting in seamlessly amongst our chaos!

A massive thank you to Zoe for being instrumental in making this book happen!

My life is one constant mental breakdown and stress factory at the best of times and throwing a follow up to my *Sunday Times* bestselling debut book into the mix only amplifies that, so a huge thank you to those around me who have to deal with the fallout from me constantly pushing myself! Notably my parents, sister Samantha, the bakery babes, Florence and whichever men I'm in a texting phase with at the time.

Also (just chucking it in here to increase my chances of being taken again) a massive thanks to those on a little Disneyworld trip with me that helped to provide much inspiration for bakes in this book. Going often would, technically, be helping me out a lot!

And, as always, me x

INDEX

air fryer spring rolls 135
almond (flaked), apple crumble + custard cheesecake 165
almond (ground)
   almond croissant loaf cake **58**, 59
   frangipane filling 59
   Snickers cake 173
   sour cherry + chocolate gelato cake 171–2
   treacle tart 188
apple
   apple crumble + custard cheesecake **164**, 165
   apple pie + custard cake 110–12, **111**

bacon
   cranberry, Brie + bacon rolls 132–4, **133**
   quiche Lorraine 123
Baileys
   Baileys custard **28**, 29
   Baileys custard tart 162, **163**
basil 125, 129, 135
Biscoff
   Biscoff blondies 52, **53**
   Biscoff poke cake 166
   Biscoff rocky road cheesecake **108**, 109
biscuits
   cheese **140**, 141
   see also digestive biscuits; Hobnob biscuits; shortbread
blondies
   Biscoff blondies 52, **53**
   churros blondies **72**, 73
   Nutella blondie roll **76**, 77
   raspberry + lemon cheesecake blondies 80, **81**
   ultimate blondies 39
blueberry + lemon cheesecake cake **114**, 115
Brie, cranberry + bacon rolls 132–4, **133**
brownies 13
   Dairy Milk millionaire brownies 113
   espresso martini hot fudge brownie sundaes 179, **180**–1
   Nutella brownies 70, **71**
   seashell brownies **46**, 47
   triple chocolate brownie cake 167–8, **169**
butter 9
buttercream
   cinnamon **54**, 55
   custard flavoured 110–12, **111**, 198, **199**
   honey **200**, 201
   lemon **114**, 115
   Milkybar funfetti **92**, 93
   ombré 158–61, **159–60**
   salted caramel **102**, 103–4
   vanilla 158–61, **159–60**

cakes
   almond croissant loaf cake 58, **59**
   apple pie + custard cake 110–12, **111**
   Biscoff poke cake 166
   blueberry + lemon cheesecake cake **114**, 115
   carrot cake 184, **185**
   chocolate orange loaf cake 196, **197**
   Earl Grey + lavender cake 74, **75**
   failure to rise 13
   pecan pie + salted caramel cake **102**, 103–4
   plum crumble cake 198, **199**
   pre-icing cooling times 13
   pumpkin spice cake **54**, 55
   raspberry ombré cheesecake cake 158–61, **159–60**
   Snickers cake 173
   sour cherry + chocolate gelato cake **170**, 171–2
   toasted honey, pear + cinnamon cake **200**, 201
   triple chocolate brownie cake 167–8, **169**
caprese quiche 125
caramel
   creamy caramel **20**, 21, 192
   Galaxy caramel lump **50**, 51
   Milkybar + Mini Egg cookie
   millionaires **68**, 69
   millionaire's shortbread 38
   millionaire's shortbread cheesecake 96, **97**
   peanut caramel 173
   pistachio cookie millionaires 87
   Snickers cake 173
   sticky toffee tart **98**, 99
   thiccc caramel 22, 38, **50**, 51, 69, 70, 87, 113, 173
   see also salted caramel
carrot cake 184, **185**
cereal, cookie 60, **61**

chai latte custard **28**, 30
Cheddar cheese
   cheese biscuits **140**, 141
   hot honey, jalapeño + cheesy garlic knots **146**, 147
   ploughman's spring rolls 135
   quiche Lorraine 123
cheese
   cheese biscuits **140**, 141
   cranberry, Brie + bacon rolls 132–4, **133**
   pear, prosciutto, gorgonzola + walnut quiche 126–7
   pumpkin, walnut, sausage + blue cheese pies **142**, 143
   roasted fig, prosciutto + truffle Boursin tart 144, **145**
   roasted grape + goats' cheese scones 124
   wild garlic, spinach, ricotta + Lancashire cheese puffs **136**, 137, **138**–9
   see also Cheddar cheese; cream cheese; mascarpone; mozzarella
cheesecake
   apple crumble + custard cheesecake **164**, 165
   Biscoff rocky road cheesecake **108**, 109
   blueberry + lemon cheesecake cake **114**, 115
   millionaire's shortbread cheesecake 96, **97**
   piña colada pie 105–7, **106**
   raspberry + lemon cheesecake blondies 80, **81**
   raspberry ombré cheesecake cake 158–61, **159–60**
   raspberry ripple cheesecake sandwiches 78, **79**
cherry *see* sour cherry
chocolate
   baked cookie dough 157
   chocolate cookie dough 56, **57**
   chocolate fudge cookies **190**, 191
   chocolate fudge sauce 31
   chocolate gelato **186**, 187
   chocolate rocky road tower **36**, 37
   cookie cereal 60
   Dairy Milk millionaire brownies 113
   Galaxy caramel lump **50**, 51
   ganache **46**, 47, 83, 96, 167–8, **169**
   Nutella blondie roll 77
   salted caramel cornflake rocky road 66
   salted caramel cornflake sandwiches 192
   Snickers cake 173

triple chocolate brownie cake 167–8, **169**
triple chocolate cornflake roll **82**, 83
see also dark chocolate; white chocolate
churros blondies **72**, 73
cinnamon
　apple crumble + custard cheesecake **164**, 165
　carrot cake 184
　churros blondies 73
　cinnamon buttercream 55
　pumpkin spice + caramelized white chocolate cookies 44
　pumpkin spice cake 55
　toasted honey, pear + cinnamon cake **200**, 201
cloves 44, 55, 184
coconut cream filling 105–7, **106**
coffee
　espresso martini hot fudge brownie sundaes 179, **180**–1
　pistachio tiramisu 152–3
condensed milk
　Biscoff poke cake 166
　caramel 96, 99
　chocolate fudge sauce 31
　thiccc caramel 22
cookie cereal 60, **61**
cookie dough
　baked cookie dough **156**, 157
　chocolate cookie dough 56, **57**
cookies
　chocolate fudge cookies **190**, 191
　Milkybar + Mini Egg cookie millionaires **68**, 69
　Milkybar funfetti cookie sandwiches **92**, 93
　oat + choc chip cookies 41, **43**
　over-spreading 13–14
　peaches + cream stuffed thiccc cookies 84–6, **85**
　pistachio cookie millionaires 87
　pumpkin spice + caramelized white chocolate cookies 44, **45**
　strawberry milkshake cookies 40, **42**
　tahini, dark chocolate + sesame cookies **194**, 195
cornflakes
　salted caramel cornflake rocky road 66, **67**
　salted caramel cornflake sandwiches 192, **193**
　triple chocolate cornflake roll **82**, 83
coulis, raspberry 78, **79**

cranberry, Brie + bacon rolls 132–4, **133**
cream (clotted), peaches + cream stuffed thiccc cookies 84–6
cream (double)
　apple crumble + custard cheesecake 165
　Baileys custard tart 162
　Biscoff ganache 52
　Biscoff poke cake 166
　Biscoff rocky road cheesecake 109
　blueberry + lemon cheesecake cake 115
　caprese quiche 125
　chai latte custard 30
　chocolate gelato 187
　coconut cream filling 105–7, **106**
　creamy caramel **20**, 21
　espresso martini hot fudge brownie sundaes 179
　ganache 46, 47, 69, 83, 93, 96, 167–8, 173, 192, **193**, 196, **197**
　Milkybar ganache 69, 93
　millionaire's shortbread cheesecake 96
　pear, prosciutto, gorgonzola + walnut quiche 126–7
　piña colada pie 105–7
　pistachio tart 100
　quiche Lorraine 123
　raspberry + lemon cheesecake blondies 80
　raspberry ombré cheesecake cake 158–61
　raspberry ripple cheesecake sandwiches 78
　rich custard 29
　salted caramel 23
　sour cherry + chocolate gelato cake 171–2
　sticky toffee sauce 26, 27
cream (soured), cheese biscuits **140**, 141
cream cheese
　apple crumble + custard cheesecake 165
　Biscoff rocky road cheesecake 109
　blueberry + lemon cheesecake cake 115
　cream cheese icing 184, **185**
　millionaire's shortbread cheesecake 96
　piña colada pie 105–7
　pistachio frosting 94–5
　pumpkin, walnut, sausage + blue cheese pies 143
　raspberry + lemon cheesecake blondies 80
　raspberry ombré cheesecake cake 158–61
　raspberry ripple cheesecake

sandwiches 78
　roasted fig, prosciutto + truffle Boursin tart 144, **145**
croissants, almond croissant loaf cake 58, **59**
crumble
　apple crumble + custard cheesecake **164**, 165
　plum crumble cake 198, **199**
curd
　lemon **24**, 25, 80, 115
　pineapple 25, 105–7
custard
　apple crumble + custard cheesecake **164**, 165
　apple pie + custard cake 110–12, **111**
　Baileys custard **28**, 29
　Baileys custard tart 162, **163**
　chai latte custard **28**, 30
　plum crumble cake 198
　rich custard **28**, 29, 165
　three ways **28**, 29–30

Dairy Milk millionaire brownies 113
dark chocolate
　chocolate fudge cookies **190**, 191
　chocolate orange loaf cake 196, **197**
　espresso martini hot fudge brownie sundaes 179, **180**–1
　ganache 83, 167–8, 173, 192, **193**, 196, **197**
　millionaire's shortbread 38
　Nutella brownies 70, **71**
　oat + choc chip cookies 41, **43**
　seashell brownies **46**, 47
　sour cherry + chocolate gelato cake **170**, 171–2
　tahini, dark chocolate + sesame cookies **194**, 195
　triple chocolate brownie cake 167–8, **169**
　triple chocolate cornflake roll **82**, 83
date(s)
　sticky toffee pudding 182
　sticky toffee tart 99
digestive biscuits
　chocolate rocky road tower 37
　Galaxy caramel lump 51
　raspberry ripple cheesecake sandwiches 78

Earl Grey + lavender cake 74, **75**
egg(s) 9

espresso martini hot fudge brownie sundaes 179, **180–1**

feta cheese, cheese biscuits **140**, 141
fig, roasted fig, prosciutto + truffle Boursin tart 144, **145**
focaccia, pepperoni pizza **128**, 129
food colourings 10
frangipane
  almond **58**, 59
  pistachio 100, **101**
frosting, pistachio 94–5

Galaxy caramel lump **50**, 51
ganache **46**, 47, 83, 96, 167–8, **169**, 173, 192, **193**, 196, **197**
  Biscoff 52, **52**
  Milkybar 69, **92**, 93
garlic, hot honey, jalapeño + cheesy garlic knots **146**, 147
gelato
  chocolate gelato **186**, 187
  sour cherry + chocolate gelato cake **170**, 171–2
ginger 44, 55
glaze, strawberry 40
goats' cheese + roasted grape scones 127
gorgonzola, pear, prosciutto + walnut quiche 124–5
grape, roasted grape + goats' cheese scones 12

ham
  ploughman's spring rolls 135
  see also prosciutto
harissa sausage rolls **130**, 131
hazelnut
  apple crumble + custard cheesecake 165
  Nutella blondie roll 77
Hobnob biscuits, Nutella brownies 70
honey
  hot honey, jalapeño + cheesy garlic knots **146**, 147
  nougat 173
  toasted honey, pear + cinnamon cake **200**, 201

icing
  pre-icing cooling times 13
  vanilla cream cheese 184, **185**
  see also buttercream; frosting
Italian meringue 105–7, **106**

jalapeño, cheesy garlic + hot honey knots **146**, 147
jars, sterilisation 13

lavender + Earl Grey cake 74, **75**
lemon
  blueberry + lemon cheesecake cake **114**, 115
  lemon curd **24**, 25, 80, 115
  raspberry + lemon cheesecake blondies 80, **81**

Mars bars, chocolate rocky road tower **36**, 37
marshmallow 13
  Biscoff rocky road cheesecake 109
  chocolate rocky road tower 37
  peanut butter crispy clusters 48
  salted caramel cornflake rocky road 66
  salted caramel cornflake sandwiches 192
  triple chocolate cornflake roll 83
mascarpone
  espresso martini hot fudge brownie sundaes 179
  pistachio tiramisu 152–3
  sour cherry + chocolate gelato cake 171–2
meringue, Italian 105–7, **106**
Milky War, chocolate rocky road tower **36**, 37
Milkybar
  Milkybar + Mini Egg cookie millionaires **68**, 69
  Milkybar funfetti cookie sandwiches **92**, 93
  Milkybar ganache 69
millionaires
  Dairy Milk millionaire brownies 113
  Milkybar + Mini Egg cookie millionaires **68**, 69
  millionaire's shortbread 38
  millionaire's shortbread cheesecake 96, **97**
  pistachio cookie millionaires 87
Mini Egg + Milkybar cookie millionaires **68**, 69
mozzarella
  caprese quiche 125
  pepperoni pizza focaccia 129
  pepperoni pizza spring rolls 135
Munchies, salted caramel cornflake rocky road 66

nougat **36**, 37, 173
Nutella
  Nutella brownies 70, **71**
  seashell brownies **46**, 47
nutmeg 44, 55, 184

oat(s)
  apple crumble + custard cheesecake **164**, 165
  oat + choc chip cookies 41, **43**
orange chocolate loaf cake 196, **197**

pastry
  Baileys custard tart 162, **163**
  piña colada pie 105–7, **106**
  pistachio tart 100, **101**
  sticky toffee tart **98**, 99
  treacle tart 188, **189**
  walnut pastry 126–7
  see also puff pastry; shortcrust pastry case
peaches + cream stuffed thiccc cookies 84–6, **85**
peanut butter crispy clusters 48, **49**
peanut caramel 173
pear
  pear, prosciutto, gorgonzola + walnut quiche 126–7
  toasted honey, pear + cinnamon cake **200**, 201
pecan nut
  carrot cake 184
  pecan pie + salted caramel cake **102**, 103–4
pepperoni
  pepperoni pizza focaccia **128**, 129
  pepperoni pizza spring rolls 135
pies
  piña colada pie 105–7, **106**
  pumpkin, walnut, sausage + blue cheese pies **142**, 143
piña colada pie 105–7, **106**
pineapple curd 25, 105–7
pistachio
  pistachio cookie millionaires 87
  pistachio frangipane 100, **101**
  pistachio rolls 94–5
  pistachio tart 100, **101**
  pistachio tiramisu 152–3, **154–5**
pizza
  pepperoni pizza focaccia **128**, 129
  pepperoni pizza spring rolls 135
ploughman's spring rolls 135
plum crumble cake 198, **199**
prosciutto

pear, prosciutto, gorgonzola + walnut quiche 124–5
roasted fig, prosciutto + truffle Boursin tart 144, **145**
puff pastry 121
   harissa sausage rolls **130**, 131
   pumpkin, walnut, sausage + blue cheese pies **142**, 143
   roasted fig, prosciutto + truffle Boursin tart 144, **145**
   wild garlic, spinach, ricotta + Lancashire cheese puffs **136**, 137, **138–9**
pumpkin
   pumpkin, walnut, sausage + blue cheese pies **142**, 143
   pumpkin spice + caramelized white chocolate cookies 44, **45**
   pumpkin spice cake **54**, 55

quiche
   caprese quiche 126
   pear, prosciutto, gorgonzola + walnut quiche 124–5
   quiche Lorraine **122**, 123
raspberry
   raspberry + lemon cheesecake blondies 80, **81**
   raspberry coulis 78, **79**
   raspberry ombré cheesecake cake 158–61, **159–60**
   raspberry ripple cheesecake sandwiches 78, **79**
Reese's, peanut butter crispy clusters 48, **49**
ricotta, Lancashire cheese, wild garlic + spinach puffs **136**, 137, **138–9**
rocky road
   Biscoff rocky road cheesecake **108**, 109
   chocolate rocky road tower **36**, 37
   salted caramel cornflake rocky road 66, **67**
rolls, cranberry, Brie + bacon 132–4, **133**
Rolos, salted caramel cornflake rocky road 66
rum, piña colada pie 105–7
salt 9
salted caramel 23
   pecan pie + salted caramel cake **102**, 103–4
   salted caramel cornflake rocky road 66, **67**
   salted caramel cornflake sandwiches 192, **193**

triple chocolate cornflake roll 83
sauces
   chocolate fudge 31
   sticky toffee 26, **27**
sausage
   harissa sausage rolls **130**, 131
   pumpkin, walnut, sausage + blue cheese pies **142**, 143
scones, roasted grape + goats' cheese 124
sesame, tahini + dark chocolate cookies **194**, 195
shallot 123, 126–7, 131
shortbread
   millionaire's shortbread 38
   millionaire's shortbread cheesecake 96, **97**
shortcrust pastry case 120
   caprese quiche 125
   quiche Lorraine **122**, 123
slicing bakes 12
Snickers cake 173
sour cherry + chocolate gelato cake **170**, 171–2
spinach, wild garlic, ricotta + Lancashire cheese puffs **136**, 137, **138–9**
sponge fingers 152–3, **154–5**
spotted dick traybake 178
spring rolls
   air fryer 135
   pepperoni pizza 135
   ploughman's 135
sterilisation techniques 13
sticky toffee pudding 182, **183**
sticky toffee sauce 26, **27**
sticky toffee tart **98**, 99
storing bakes 13
strawberry
   strawberry glaze 40
   strawberry milkshake cookies 40, **42**
suet puddings, spotted dick traybake 178
sundaes, espresso martini hot fudge brownie 179, **180–1**
syrup, orange 196, **197**
tahini, dark chocolate + sesame cookies **194**, 195
tarts
   Baileys custard 162, **163**
   pistachio 100, **101**
   roasted fig, prosciutto + truffle Boursin 144, **145**
   sticky toffee **98**, 99
   treacle 188, **189**
thermometers 10
tins 10
   lining 12

tiramisu, pistachio 152–3, **154–5**
toffee *see* sticky toffee
tomato, caprese quiche 125
traybake, spotted dick 178
treacle
   sticky toffee pudding 182
   sticky toffee tart 99
   treacle tart 188, **189**
troubleshooting 13–14
truffle Boursin, roasted fig + prosciutto tart 144, **145**

vanilla 9
   vanilla buttercream 158–61, **159–60**
   vanilla cream cheese icing 184, **185**

walnut
   carrot cake 184
   pear, prosciutto, gorgonzola + walnut quiche 124–5
   pumpkin, walnut, sausage + blue cheese pies **142**, 143
   walnut pastry 126–7
white chocolate
   Biscoff blondies 52
   Biscoff ganache 52
   Biscoff rocky road cheesecake **108**, 109
   churros blondies **72**, 73
   ganache **46**, 47, 83, 167–8
   peaches + cream stuffed thiccc cookies 84–6
   pistachio cookie millionaires 87
   pumpkin spice + caramelized white chocolate cookies 44, **45**
   raspberry + lemon cheesecake blondies 80, **81**
strawberry milkshake cookies 40
ultimate blondies 39
wild garlic, spinach, ricotta + Lancashire cheese puffs **136**, 137, **138–9**

First published in Great Britain in 2025
by Yellow Kite
An imprint of Hodder & Stoughton
An Hachette UK company

1

Copyright © George Hepher 2025
Photography copyright © Kimberly Espinel 2025

The right of George Hepher to be identified as the Author of the Work has been asserted by him in accordance with the Copyright, Designs and Patents Act 1988.

All rights reserved. No part of this publication may be reproduced, stored in a retrieval system, or transmitted, in any form or by any means without the prior written permission of the publisher, nor be otherwise circulated in any form of binding or cover other than that in which it is published and without a similar condition being imposed on the subsequent purchaser. A CIP catalogue record for this title is available from the British Library

Hardback ISBN: 9781529442151
eBook ISBN: 9781529442168

Senior Commissioning Editor: Nicole Thomas
Senior Project Editor: Charlotte Macdonald
Designer: Studio Polka
Photography: Kimberly Espinel
Food Stylist: Katie Marshall and Rosie French

Colour origination by Alta Image London
Printed and bound in China by C&C Offset Printing Co Ltd
Hodder & Stoughton policy is to use papers that are natural, renewable and recyclable products and made from wood grown in sustainable forests. The logging and manufacturing processes are expected to conform to the environmental regulations of the country of origin.

Yellow Kite
Hodder & Stoughton Ltd
Carmelite House
50 Victoria Embankment
London
EC4Y 0DZ

www.yellowkitebooks.co.uk
www.hodder.co.uk